To Jim & Kaede
Best wishes
Jeff Hutchins
Dec. 2005

A Press Conference with God

*An Atheist Talks to God
and Gets Answers to Your Questions*

By Jeffrey Melvin Hutchins

Copyright © 2005 by Jeffrey Melvin Hutchins

ISBN 0-7414-2872-5

Published by:

INFINITY
PUBLISHING.COM

1094 New DeHaven Street, Suite 100
West Conshohocken, PA 19428-2713
Info@buybooksontheweb.com
www.buybooksontheweb.com
Toll-free (877) BUY BOOK
Local Phone (610) 941-9999
Fax (610) 941-9959

Printed in the United States of America

Printed on Recycled Paper

Published October 2005

For Rachel and Nell
Whose goodness shines with the glow
of independent thought

Table of Contents

FOREWORD by DR. JOYCE STARR

INTRODUCTION by JEFFREY MELVIN HUTCHINS

I. JEREMIAH'S OPENING STATEMENT

II. BEING GOD
1. God, who are you? What are you? Are you real?
2. Is God a man or a woman, or some other gender?
3. What is God's favorite cookie?
4. What do you do on your day off, God?
5. What does God do for fun? Does God have a hobby?
6. What's a typical day in the life of God?
7. Does God sleep?
8. Does God age?
9. Can God speak every language?
10. How does God communicate messages to mankind? To what extent can the understanding of man comprehend God?
11. How can we contact God?
12. When can I meet you, God?
13. Why is there so much confusion about God's existence?
14. As an agnostic, I cannot really know if God exists. Does God have a similar problem? God, are you sure that you are God? Is there only one of you?
15. Why isn't life getting any better? Why couldn't you have made things a little bit easier on all of us down here? Why disease? Why hate? Why rape and murder and lying and mosquitoes and rotten fruit and floods and famine? Do you really love us? Why did you create us? And if you can't answer these questions, if I can never know the answers, then why did you make me capable of asking them?
16. Is God omniscient and omnipotent? If so, then why do people have to suffer? If the answer is no, then why do people believe God is? Either way, does it matter?
17. Is God all good?
18. Do you feel people expect too much of God?

19. What does God think of atheists?
20. Is it lonely being the only God?
21. How did God come to be God? Where did God come from?
22. Who is God's mother?
23. Can you give us a biography of God?
24. If God is without attributes, how are our objectifying minds supposed to know God?
25. Is there always the same God? Can someone new become God?
26. Who or what can replace God?
27. Where did God dwell before the birth of the universe?
28. Where does God live now? Does he have a wife?
29. Who is God's God? Who does God answer to?
30. Can God procrastinate?
31. How should we worship God?
32. Some people say that God is love. Is that true?
33. It is said that "cleanliness is next to Godliness." Is *this* true?
34. Since God is so powerful and magnificent, why would God stoop to destroy an insignificant individual just because she doesn't believe in God? And, if God is a loving God, why would God make people burn in hell for eternity?
35. Does God demand or respond to sacrifices?
36. How did God ever get the reputation of being perfect, all-wise, all-knowing? God is supposed to be perfect, to know everything. But then, out of this perfection, God creates an imperfect universe – especially our little speck of dust, Earth. Why didn't God leave well enough alone?
37. If there is both matter and anti-matter, then is there also God and anti-God? In other words, is there a devil, a Satan that creates and controls all the bad things in the universe?
38. There are people who claim God has spoken with them, or appeared to them in a vision, or guided their hand as they wrote. Has God done those things?
39. Is it just a coincidence that "God" is "dog" spelled backwards?

40. What does God look like?
41. Why is God invisible?
42. Can God take on human form and appear among us? Has God ever done that?
43. God, why not reveal yourself in some form to the modern world in order to stop the current mayhem?
44. Where is the Goddess? We have "one nation under God," and "in God we trust." I would think the Goddess would be pretty upset by now for not getting her fair share of worship.

III. CREATION

45. Evolution or creation?
46. In the poem "Trees," Joyce Kilmer wrote, "Only God can make a tree." Is that true?
47. People say every day is a gift from God. Is it?
48. Is quantum mechanics reconcilable with relativity, and is string theory the mechanism?
49. One of the God's Billboard "quotes" from God says, "Big bang theory. You've got to be kidding." What about the "Big Bang" theory? Is it wrong?
50. Why does anything exist?
51. Why do mosquitoes exist?
52. What are God's greatest creations?
53. What was God's greatest failure or disappointment?
54. The Bible says God created the world in six days. What's the real story?
55. Is the universe expanding or contracting, and what happens to us?
56. Is there such a thing as a parallel universe?
57. So, we can never do more than speculate about other universes?
58. Why did God create humans, who only wreck all the other beautiful things on Earth?
59. God, why did you choose to create each person differently? More specifically, what is the purpose of creating such complex personalities in each individual? Was it perhaps to teach us how to love one another?

60. Was it hard to make six billion people and each one different than the other? Because sometimes there are twins.

61. Why only male and female human beings? We could have used at least two others!

62. If God did not exist, would the world go on?

63. Are humans the highest life form on Earth?

64. Why did God pick humans to have a consciousness?

65. Are we alone in the universe?

66. Is there life on other planets? If so, what kind of life?

67. Will Earthlings ever make direct contact with intelligent beings from another planet? What are they like?

68. Does God have any regret for creating us humans, considering the mess we have made of this planet and the amount of fighting we do amongst ourselves? How could God have made us better? We can't be the only beings in the universe with our ability for thought. There must be others who have managed better than we have, who aren't so petty and self-centered.

69. I'm curious what an improved human model might be like.

70. How will humans evolve in the future?

71. When God created life forms, why were digestive systems designed to make waste products? Wouldn't total absorption have been more efficient?

72. Where do the great inventions of history come from? Does God plant the ideas in the minds of the great thinkers and inventors?

73. I did not choose to be born, but I was born, naked and ignorant. I did not plan or conceive myself. All that I am, I was given; all that I know, I learned. I ask myself questions about the meaning of life, and answers seem to appear, answers I was not born knowing. Can these answers come from anyone but God, and if not from God, then does that make me greater than that which created me?

74. What inspired God to create music and humor?

75. I know, I know, I've been a bit critical of late when I think of you. Truly, your Godship, have you lost interest in the fabulous variety of your creations here? It seems you started us up and then hoped we would evolve on our own.

76. Were people created to serve and to please God?

IV. LIFE

77. Why do bad things happen to good people, and vice versa?

78. What does God consider God's greatest gift to the living?

79. What does it all mean? What is the meaning of life?

80. What is your soul?

81. Do animals have souls?

82. Why is life such a struggle?

83. Many people say everything happens for a reason. Is that true?

84. In "The Purpose-Driven Life" by Rick Warren, the opening paragraph says, "This book is dedicated to you. Before you were born, God planned *this moment* in your life. It is no accident that you are holding this book. God *longs* for you to discover the life he created you to live here on Earth, and forever in eternity." My question is, is this true?

85. Some people say there are no "accidents," that people secretly want the accident to happen. Are there really accidents?

86. We call many things that happen together a "coincidence." Do these things happen by mistake or by your design?

87. Are all the myriad occurrences on our planet part of a learning process especially geared to humans, and if so, to what end?

88. Why does God treat old people so badly?

89. Where are my unmatched socks?

90. Do people have a destiny or predetermined fate?

91. Does history repeat itself?

92. Do you give us just one lifetime to do it right, or do you give us as many as it takes to do it right?

93. When will there be world peace?
94. I understand God can't make predictions, but can God tell us whether there *might be* peace in the Middle East? Is it possible?
95. Do you weep when people kill non-human creatures for sport?
96. Is humankind doomed to destroy itself? Will we destroy Earth?
97. Then how far will human beings advance? What changes would God like to see?
98. Okay, so... *does* God care about me?
99. Is time travel possible?
100. Why does time seem to change? When we are young, it seems to go slowly, and when we are old, it seems to speed up.
101. Why isn't the world perfect?
102. What surprises you most about humans?
103. Are people inherently good, inherently bad, or neither?
104. I was raised in a traditional religion. I realize there is a "force" that is a part of me. It is not part of my physical body or my conscious mind. I live in a three-dimensional world, but I sense another force beyond those three dimensions. It is there. I have experienced altered states of consciousness. What is this force?

V. DEATH AND DYING

105. A friend suggested that we all have free will before we come to Earth, that is, we choose those experiences that we will have during this life. I bought that. Then he said, "I believe that all of the men and women who perished on 9/11 chose that experience." So, my question is, do we really have free will? Are matters of our life preordained? Do people perish and suffer because they willed it?
106. Why does aging scare people so much?
107. Why can't death be painless?
108. Well, why *does* everything God makes die? Why don't people live forever?

109. Is it fair you live forever, God, while we your children perish? Why, Creator, endlessly destroy your own creation?
110. What is death?
111. Why do all life forms fight death and struggle to stay alive, particularly people who believe that death will bring union with God?
112. Why do people die seemingly before their time?
113. Is there life after death?
114. Can our loved ones see us in some way after they die?
115. So I will never see my dear departed mother/uncle/spouse/friend again?
116. How can I get to heaven?
117. Is there a place called hell? If so, what is it like?
118. Is there purgatory, a place where dead souls are judged?
119. If there is no heaven or hell, what is the motivation for people to be good in this life?
120. Shouldn't people be afraid that they might go to hell if they are evil or don't worship God?
121. Do we know people from past lives?
122. Are there ghosts?
123. Wait a minute! A great many people, including lots of honest, sincere people, have seen ghosts or apparitions. If there are no ghosts, what did they see? Were they lying?
124. Where is the hope for those who know that love is stronger than death, when death separates those who love each other?
125. Why in the world does God make the lifespan of dogs so short? That's a very bad decision!

VI. RELIGION

126. Are you also the press secretary for Jesus and the Holy Spirit?
127. Your boss is known by many names and worshipped with many different rituals. Is there a name God likes best and a ritual that is highly expressive of God's nature?

128. How does God feel about the criticism and parodies of religion and of God by Monty Python, Mel Brooks, and others?

129. I have wondered if God has a support office! We portray angels as doing God's work in our realm. Are there "agents" we can enlist to facilitate our efforts on Earth?

130. Why should I believe in God? What evidence is there that God exists?

131. Is it okay not to believe in God?

132. I am confident that there is not a God and that humans make this stuff up for various reasons. I am respectful of this Earth, my fellow people, and the interdependent web of all existence. Why do churches exist, with all their money, power and rules, to sell the idea that God exists and can help?

133. What are some origins of faith?

134. What is the difference between a cult and a religion?

135. What is truth?

136. God's books – the Bible, Torah and Koran – that are easily misunderstood, have resulted in Christianity, Judaism, and Islam having caused more woe in the world than anything else. What defense does God have?

137. Okay, so who wrote the Bible?

138. Why are there so many religions, and how do we know which one to believe in and follow?

139. If, as you say, most religions are wrong in their core beliefs, should they stop what they're doing? Should there be just one religion? Wouldn't God's job be easier?

140. We all know Jesus was Jewish and that he celebrated the Jewish tradition of Passover the night before he was crucified. Yet the people who follow Jesus reject Jewish tradition and call themselves Christians. So my question is, if Jesus were alive today, what religion would he be?

141. Was Jesus really the son of God?

142. Who are these Christ-like people today?

143. How many "saviors" are there in God's kingdom that you can furnish to newly discovered civilizations?

144. Who was right – Jesus Christ, Buddha, Muhammad, or someone else?

145. Has God sent prophets to Earth or spoken to people and told them what to say to everyone else? If so, are there any prophets on Earth today?

146. Does God ever put images of Jesus or Mary or any other religious person on walls, in food, or any other place people might find it?

147. It seems as if the human conception of God is changing. Should it change, and if so, how should it? What should our conception be?

148. Can people be "born again?" Does God desire this?

149. What do you think of fundamentalists of any religion?

150. Didn't God know in advance Adam and Eve would disobey him?

151. Did God ask Noah to build the ark?

152. Did God write the Ten Commandments?

153. Are there angels?

154. Did God bring the children of Israel out of Egypt?

155. Is there such a thing as the Holy Grail? If so, what is it and where is it?

156. Are there miracles?

157. We've read about some of the ancient events and attitudes that made God angry. Are there new topics or types of things that weren't around when the holy books were being written that we should watch out for?

158. What does God think of the crusades and other religious wars?

159. Do we need to be saved? If so, from what?

160. Does God listen to prayers?

161. You haven't said whether God is influenced by prayer, or did God set everything in motion and sit back and let it happen through natural law?

162. Can prayer help the person who is praying or other people not even in the room?

163. Do faith healers actually work?

164. There have been many prophets throughout time; how does one differentiate between the minor prophets and those who were founders of independent faiths?

165. If all religions "have it wrong," what do you think of the ministers, rabbis, priests, mullahs, and others who speak for these religions?

166. What does God think of religious schools?

167. We've been thinking about who should be authorized to study and spread your word. Does God have trouble with women, gay people, or youngsters being priests?

168. Many people ask God, "Why?" But I'd like to ask, "Why not?"

169. Oh Lord, God of Heaven and Earth, we worship and praise your grace. Please show us your will in our lives and in a way that we can understand. Please watch over and protect our children and help us to teach them in your love. Your goodness and grace are beyond our comprehension; please grant us a glimpse of your greatness so that our faith may be strong.

VII. WAR AND OTHER NASTY BEHAVIOR

170. How do you explain war?

171. How does a good God account for the evil in the world?

172. Is killing another person ever justified?

173. What about killing oneself? How does God feel about suicide?

174. Is it morally defensible to kill bugs? As I was gardening, there were ants and spiders and some other creepy-crawlies... I killed them all – no one was spared. Now, I know ants don't hurt me, and while spiders scare the bejezus out of me, I know they are supposed to be good for the garden. But frankly, I just don't care. I squash them all. I wouldn't kill a cat or dog or even a squirrel, and would let mice be (as long as they are outside!). But what is it about bugs? Their size? Their appearance? Am I a bug Hitler?

175. Whose side is God on in war? How does God decide whom to support?

176. Do you have any thoughts on how to stop all of those idiots who claim to be doing God's will? The most obvious example, of course, is that of waging war and killing people in God's name.

177. Why do humans fight with each other so much? What is that about?

178. So much violence and killing are done in God's name. Why doesn't God step forward and declare an end to this madness before we are all annihilated?

179. What are God's thoughts about war? Is it ever justified?

180. Is there such a thing as a good war?

181. Are there interplanetary wars elsewhere in the universe?

182. Does the number 666 mean anything to you?

183. God, what would you like to say to the world today, especially about the problems, injustices, and divisions that are so evident?

184. (From the book "Faxes to God," a series of related questions)
    - For a merciful God, haven't you been hard on the Jews?
    - If we are the chosen people, why are we mostly chosen for hatred and anti-semitism?
    - Why did you let Hitler kill all those Jews in the holocaust?
    - I ask why the holocaust happened, and why did you not do anything about it?
    - If you helped Moses out of slavery, why didn't you help Jews in World War II?

VIII. CULTURE AND SOCIETY

185. Can God make no one homeless or sick?

186. Will I ever find someone to love me?

187. Where does happiness lie?

188. Why do girls not like boys and boys not like girls?

189. Should we be trying to protect our environment, and if so how?

190. Is God a member of the Green Party?
191. What did God think of the CBS television program "Joan of Arcadia?"
192. What is God's favorite song?
193. What about rap music?
194. Are there any movies or TV shows God favors?
195. Name some movies that God would "like."
196. Are there movies that God would probably dislike?
197. So much art tries to depict God or religious themes. What art is God's favorite? Does any of it get it right?
198. Is "The Da Vinci Code" correct? Did Jesus marry Mary Magdalene? Did they have a child? Is that her on Jesus' right in "The Last Supper?"
199. Are there any people you don't like?
200. Who will win the next presidential election?
201. Did God guide George Washington and arrange events to form the United States of America?
202. Does astrology work?
203. Can meditation help us to reach God?
204. Many people do good things in God's name. Does that please God?
205. What impresses God the most – charitable acts of atheists or those of believers hoping for a reward?
206. Why is it that some people seem to have everything – good health, good looks, lots of money, happy lives – and others seem to have so little?
207. Theologian Reinhold Niebuhr wrote, "Modern Western civilization may perish because it falsely worshiped technology as a final good." Is he correct?
208. What does God think the deal is with George Bush and the right-wingers?
209. President Bush claims to go to God with the really tough questions and tries to do God's will? Has God spoken with him or with others?

IX. MORALITY

210. Are there moral absolutes? Is there such a thing as good and evil?

211. What, if anything, is a sin? Do the "seven deadly sins" really exist?
212. What about "original sin?"
213. Help us to know how to love our enemies in today's conflict with Iraq and other countries.
214. Jesus told us "love your enemies." Was he crazy?
215. How does God feel about abortion?
216. What happens to the souls of babies that are aborted?
217. Does God support capital punishment?
218. Is marriage a good thing? If so, why?
219. Are marriages made in heaven?
220. Why is my ex-husband such a jerk?
221. Why am I gay (homosexual), and why does it matter?
222. What about premarital sex, homosexuality, and other issues of morality?
223. Did God create AIDS as a way to reduce homosexuality? What is God's position on gay marriage?
224. I'm curious how our definition of love, particularly romantic love, is evolving along with everything else. Society places restraints on whom we can love and how many people we can love. We are taught very early that monogamy is king, mates should be about the same age, and so on. Are we moving toward a freer attitude about love and away from petty jealousy, possessiveness, and a very limiting view of how to love?
225. Why are people so greedy?
226. Is honesty worth all the flak we have to take for it?
227. Does God condone cloning?
228. Is God watching when we do things, especially things we should not be doing?
229. Why is the sex act, which is one of the most natural things in the world, considered so taboo by most people?
230. Is God concerned by blasphemy? What do you consider blasphemous?

X. HUMANITY

231. Does God have a favorite people or a favorite *type* of person?

232. My dear child: You are in heaven now and do not have to see the evils that man is doing to the children. The children are suffering so badly, every day new children are leaving – Polly from Petaluma, the little girl from Missouri, and all the others that were hurt and suffered. Why is life so hard for America's children? Why does God allow them to suffer?

233. What should we do, if anything, about overpopulation?

234. Is it okay to use contraceptives to control birth rates?

235. Does humankind learn from its mistakes?

236. What should humans' relationship to other creatures on Earth be? Should we eat them? Should we make them work for us? Should we have them as pets? In other words, how do you see us vis-à-vis your other creatures?

237. How is it that so often I do harm that I do not mean to do, and I fail to do the good things I intend? Every day, we betray ourselves. We break our own rules, and we deliberately say things, think things, or do things of which we are ashamed or that make us unhappy. Sometimes – as with alcohol, tobacco, sex, ambitions, or selfishness – we even destroy ourselves. Why do we not resist these temptations that cause us to deny all that we believe in, even leading us to hurt our loved ones and our friends? On the other hand, why are we often unable to accomplish the good things we wish to do?

238. Why does God let vile people procreate?

239. How does God feel about prospective parents trying to choose the sex of their children?

240. My love is everything for me. Nothing has more value for me than those I love. When everything will have disappeared, lord, who will remember the value of that love? Does love have value?

241. It seems that people no longer get worked up over big causes. Does that mean we have already evolved as a people to the point where there are no major battles to fight, like ending slavery and establishing human rights for all the people of the world?

242. How does God react when someone says, "God bless" something?

243. Does God actually "damn" people?

244. Nature shows that the predator feeds off its victim, that among animals there is no charity – the strong dominate the weak. That is essentially what Hitler said, that the Earth belongs to the strong. Was he wrong?

245. You know that saying that goes something like, "God never gives us more trouble than we can handle." Please explain. And about that "how much we can handle" part – why has God tested my limits so rigorously? Surely, our perceptions on my capacity differ vastly!

246. When I have a serious problem in my life that I can't quite fix, should I just give up and say "It's in God hands now." Or should I keep trying until I have a nervous breakdown?

247. Many people put their faith, hope, and dreams in a merciful God, a thinking God, a God like the God of the Bible. If God is not that kind of God, what should they do now?

248. But many people rely on a "higher power." For example, people in a 12-step program appeal to their higher power for strength to break the bonds of addiction. If they know that God will not intervene to help them, won't they lose hope?

249. Where do we go from here?

250. Does God have any advice for us humans?

POSTWORD from JEFFREY MELVIN HUTCHINS

ACKNOWLEDGEMENTS

INDEX

Think only on those things that are in line with your principles and can bear the full light of day. The content of your character is your choice. Day by day, what you choose, what you think, and what you do is who you become. Your integrity is your destiny - it is the light that guides your way.
    -Heraclitus

That "creativity" is beyond analysis is a romantic illusion we must now outgrow. It cannot be learned perhaps, but it can certainly be encouraged and abetted. We can put ourselves in the way of having ideas, by reading and discussion and by acquiring the habit of reflection, guided by the familiar principle that we are not likely to find answers to questions not yet formulated in the mind.
    -Sir Peter Brian Medawar

FOREWORD
By Dr. Joyce Starr

If you believe God is managing your bank account, do not buy this book!

If you believe God is angry that you put on extra weight, do not buy this book!

If you believe God is annoyed when you argue with a loved one, do not buy this book!

One so often hears the phrase, "This book has had a profound effect on my life."

However, when asked precisely HOW their lives were altered — that is, when B suddenly became A — most people can **rarely** identify a specific transformation of thought or action.

A Press Conference with God <u>has had</u> a profound effect on my life.

Until I read this wonderful book, I held the firm belief—perhaps much like YOU—that God was indeed watching my every move and that He/She had even intervened directly at critical junctures along the way.

This belief was a huge source of comfort.

I would naturally remember to thank God when events worked out in a positive manner (though admittedly, perhaps not often or loudly enough!) and fervently try to reach Him/Her when life was not moving in my preferred direction. Sooner or later – I KNEW – my call would get through. After all, God was *watching over ME!*

A Press Conference with God has forever changed my ability to conjure up such images. God is not too busy or otherwise distracted to answer my call. He/She doesn't care if I voice appreciation often or loudly enough. God will not be jogging behind me if I accidentally drop my keys and will not be keeping pace with my every future step.

Am I upset? Has my life been diminished? **NO**! Why not?

Shouldn't I be outraged by the message that God is not bagging groceries, filling my gas tank or ensuring that natural disasters will not reach <u>my</u> doorstep? Shouldn't I feel a huge sense of LOSS over the realization that God is not darting back and forth over my pillow at night like a stealth jet fighter pilot?

To the contrary! I am not upset, because this wonderful work has forever <u>enriched my life</u> by:

- Releasing me from such limited thinking and YET...

- Reinforcing my belief in a Supreme Power and Angelic forces for Good!

How can I explain such a <u>seeming</u> contradiction? This would be revealing too much.

Open the pages and begin your own personal transformation.

Dr. Joyce Starr

Dr. Starr is the author of *Faxes to God* (Harper San Francisco), *Covenant Over Middle Eastern Waters* (Henry Holt), *How To Pray On Water* (Starrcraft.Com), *How Children Pray to God at the Western Wall of Jerusalem* (Starrcraft.Com) and *Kissing Through Glass* (Contemporary Books).

INTRODUCTION
BY JEFFREY MELVIN HUTCHINS

I am an atheist, and you may be wondering, "Why would an atheist write a book about God?" The main reason is that so many people to whom I am close believe in God, that it's natural for me to think about the subject. I asked myself, "If I tried to believe in God, what kind of God could I possibly imagine?" That was the genesis (no pun intended) for this book.

We atheists have been feared and misunderstood and reviled for centuries. For most of history and in most societies, atheism has been a capital offense. Countries that barely punished rapists felt that atheists were too dangerous to be allowed to live. Apparently, thoughts are more frightening than deeds. We are seen as very *negative* people, as pessimists, always trying to take something *away* from everyone else: no prayer in school, no Nativity displays on public grounds, etc. No one ever hears the GOOD things we atheists contribute to the culture.

I call myself an OPTIMISTIC ATHEIST, which seems like an oxymoron to a lot of people. I have often been asked, "If you don't believe in God, how can you go on? How can you have hope for the future and live a moral life? Isn't it too depressing?"

The atheists I know are about the most moral people around, but I can't speak for all atheists because I don't exactly seek them out. I don't hang out in Atheist Clubs or visit Atheist Societies or wear Atheist Insignia. I am not an atheist just to be contrary. Heck, I'd have to be crazy to *choose* to be an atheist, given how much flak I get on those rare occasions I "come out" as one. I'm an atheist because none of the visions of God that I've thought about seems to stick in my brain. I'm very happy for people who believe in God and have a strong faith and a deep personal relationship with their God, but every time I've tried to believe, I realize that for me, none of it makes much sense. People don't choose beliefs from a menu of options; we believe what makes sense to us, with no claim that it should make sense for everyone else, too.

Still, I am an optimist. In fact, I find atheism very liberating, because I don't fear that a deity is planning or controlling my life. If bad things happen to me, it's not because I was bad, and if good things happen, it's not (necessarily) because I was good. So, I follow the rules – especially the Golden Rule – and live a moral life because it makes me happy and gives me a better life, not because I'm afraid that I'll be punished by some invisible dude if I'm bad. When you come right down to it, those believers who think that the only reason to be good is fear of God are not really people you'd want to bet your life on. I'd much rather depend on someone who is good because they WANT to be good.

Manifestations of God are everywhere. In the former CBS TV show, "Joan of Arcadia," God pops up as everything from a black woman in the school cafeteria to a plumber fixing the leak in Joan's family's sink. Giant billboards appear on highways all across America sporting pithy sayings attributed to God. A best-selling book relates "Conversations with God." Even DeBeers diamond ads are invoking God's creativeness. Millions of Americans are thrilled by this new focus on God. And millions of others don't know what to make of it.

A lot of the people I meet aren't quite sure where they stand with God, or at least with all this talk of God. As an atheist, I don't find it useful or believable that there is any sort of planning, thinking, organized force or deity that creates and controls the universe or anything IN the universe. But my entire life, I have been surrounded by and affected by people who have strong faith in that God, and so I have spent a lot of time thinking about what such a traditional God would really "think" if God existed. It is impossible for me to accept that such a thinking God could be the God of the Bible and of most organized religions.

In 1995, I gave a talk at the Unitarian Universalist Church of the North Hills in suburban Pittsburgh called "Who's Afraid of the Big, Bad Atheist?" in which I tried to explain why atheists have been so hated and feared throughout history, right up to today. My talk was well received, and I was asked to speak again about atheism.

I felt that my second talk should explore the subject of God (or no God) in a different way. I opted to turn the topic on its head and examine the opposite end of the spectrum. What if God could come and talk to the congregation? What would God have to say? I decided I would portray God's Press Secretary! I could still deliver the "word of God" as I imagined it, and this device gave me greater freedom in the kinds of questions I could take and the kinds of answers I could give. I called myself Jeremiah (which means "Sent by God"). I asked the congregation and other friends to tell me the questions they would like to ask God if given the chance.

This book, then, represents the words of Jeremiah speaking on behalf of God. It is especially in tune with the principles and purposes of Unitarian Universalism, a long-established faith tradition, mostly but not exclusively American, that has approximately 500,000 members in over 1000 congregations in the United States. (Thomas Jefferson and three other early presidents were unitarians.) It will also appeal to Buddhists, Taoists, Humanists, Methodists, Quakers, Atheists, and anyone else who is inquisitive and open-minded about how life began, what happens when we die, and everything in between.

3

If you are like me, you don't spend much time reading books of philosophy. Let's face it; philosophy essays can be drier than a sandstorm in the Sahara. But you may be surprised to discover that YOU are something of a philosopher. After all, a philosopher is, basically, just a person who ponders the tough questions in life and tries to make sense of the universe or some piece of it. I'll bet you do that almost daily.

This is NOT a book of philosophy, but it will deal with some very philosophical issues. It is meant first as a diversion, something to get you thinking but also enjoying life.

For this book, I created two "characters." Jeremiah is God's Press Secretary, and is prone, like most press secretaries, to poor jokes, evasive answers, and a desire to keep the press happy. A press secretary is someone who speaks on behalf of his or her boss to electronic and print reporters. The press secretary can answer questions when the boss is not available. Their answers are considered official. They represent what the boss would say if he or she were there. Members of the press ask questions, so in this case, the "press" is you and people like you.

The other "character" is God – not a human or even a living character, but simply a presence that must always be true to its nature. The answers Jeremiah gives are my version of this reality that is a product of my imagination. I do not personally believe all the answers any more than Agatha Christie believed in Miss Marple.

If you are looking for a traditional book on God that reinforces mainstream perspectives, read no further. This book is not for you. The God I envision, the God that "answers" these questions, is not mainstream.

What you are about to read is **_satire_** which, like most satire, also has a serious message to convey. I was brought up to believe that ideas – even conflicting ideas – about the nature of the universe and the relationship of all living things in the universe are open for consideration and discussion. So, please, if you are offended by anything that you read here, let me know by visiting www.apressconference.com, rather than burning something in front of my house or declaring a _fatwa_ on my head, like Salman Rushdie.

I'm reasonably sure that some people who consider themselves very religious _will_ be offended by some of my comments. That is NOT my goal. What I want to do is stimulate my readers' minds, make them think about the nature of the universe without boring the pants off them. I'd also be pleased if people who are immediately turned off by my non-traditional perspective would turn off their automatic rejection of my ideas and use this as an opportunity to reexamine some of their own beliefs. Do you think God is a benevolent, omnipotent male? Okay, I won't say you are wrong, but I will challenge you to consider another view of God. If you keep an open mind, you may just come to some new ways of thinking about your God without changing your core beliefs.

When I have performed excerpts of the Press Conference at various congregations (each of which comes up with new questions for God), I've been amazed at how some people seem to feel that my answers actually represent some official position, as if God had spoken to me. People who know better still seem to accept that there is something deeper in my answers than just the imagination of an ordinary man. Which leads me to believe that the major religious texts of our world – the Bible, the Torah, the Koran, and the I Ching, among others – benefited from this same suspension of disbelief. Perhaps the original tellers of the tales in these books knew full well that they were just stories, but the first listeners fell under the spell of a tale well told, and began to believe there was divine inspiration for the words. Maybe the storytellers themselves began to believe it as well. Certainly, it is an easy temptation to question the source of one's own inspiration. Why not believe that God spoke to you, or *through* you? Perhaps "spoke" is too literal a word. "Put those ideas in your head" is more like it.

The answers from "God" are presented according to various categories, specifically: Being God, Creation, Life, Death and Dying, Religion, War and Other Nasty Behavior, Culture and Society, Morality, and Humanity. I do not expect you to read through all the answers in order, but rather to jump to those questions that have the most meaning for you. The answers to some questions are intertwined with other answers in different chapters, so it is imperative that certain information be repeated to make sure that internal consistency is maintained and that you are not left scratching your head too often.

Questions came to me phrased two different ways. Some people asked their question directly to God. "Are YOU real?" "What if YOU did not exist?" Other people directed their question to the press secretary. "How does God communicate?" I have left all the questions intact except to make them read more like a real press conference.

Through Jeremiah, I can answer questions *about* God in addition to answering questions *on behalf of* God. That's an important freedom, because people have so many questions about God, much the way the White House press secretary is asked about his or her boss. ("How is the president feeling today?" "Is he upset about what the senator said?")

One final note to the careful reader: You will observe that I never give God a gender. I never say "He" or "She" or "Him" or "Hers." (And I never resort to the hideous "It.") God is just God. There is nothing more to say that does not bias the answer. If you want to know more about this issue, read the chapter on Being God.

And so, I will now turn the podium over to Jeremiah to reveal the answers to your questions. The press conference is about to begin. You've each been given a special Press Pass. Please enter the auditorium quietly and find your seats.

– Jeffrey Melvin Hutchins

A Press Conference with God

I. THE OPENING STATEMENT

Welcome, ladies and gentlemen. My name is Jeremiah. I am Press Secretary to the Almighty. I am delighted to be with you today. Please take your seats so we can begin the press conference. We want to take as many of your questions as time permits. Before we begin, I have a statement I'd like to read.

The reason that you've never heard of a press conference with God before is that there has never been one. God has intervened in human history only once, and fully intended never to do so again. However, the recent epidemic of people speaking for God and their bald-faced attempts to state that their desires are God's desires has forced God to direct me to conduct this unique one-time-only event. We cannot emphasize enough that there is no human being – or any other inhabitant of Earth for that matter – that is authorized to speak for God.

Here are the ground rules for the press conference:

You may ask God any question you want on any subject. Please don't bother giving us your name; we can easily look it up later. You are each allowed one question, and, if need be, one follow-up based on the answer. We know some of the questions you have because you sent them as faxes to be placed in the Western Wall in Jerusalem and they ended up in the book "Faxes to God" assembled by Dr. Joyce Starr. Those questions will be marked by an asterisk (*). They will be collected, along with the rest of your questions, and presented in a book according to their category.

There are certain questions we will not answer. We are not here to do your homework for you and give you answers to questions you can deduce yourself. We will not be solving any mysteries for you, either, such as who really killed John

Kennedy or what happened to Jimmy Hoffa. We can't predict the future and won't even try, although we can tell you about the experience of other planets like yours that faced similar situations.

We won't be... yes, sir? Yes, you in the second row. What's that?... No, God will *not* be making a surprise appearance today. Any of you who came here expecting to see God might as well leave now and give your seat to someone else.

Ma'am, you have a question for me? You want to know how I will get the answers from God if God is not here? Well, all I can tell you is that those of us in the Administration are well versed in the basics. I feel confident I will be able to answer pretty much everything you want to know based on my lengthy service with God. How long? Let's just say I remember when your great-great grandmother was born and leave it at that.

Any other questions for me? All right, then, let's get started. Just let me know if anything else pops up. I have all the time in the world, and I do mean ALL the time in the world, but unfortunately, you all just have one lifetime to get through this. So, here we go.

II. BEING GOD
Or, WHAT'S A NICE INFINITE BEING LIKE YOU DOING IN A COSMOS LIKE THIS?

It was a relatively easy decision as to which category of questions to use first. It's a good idea for you to get some background on God before you begin to ponder God's answers about creation, war, ethics, etc.

Often, it's younger people who are concerned with questions about the nature of God. For example, the question about God's favorite cookie came from a 10-year-old boy. Questions like this are intriguing, because in the innocence with which they are asked, they imply much deeper thought than if they came, tongue in cheek, from an adult human.

The first question is also from a child, a 9-year-old girl, and that made it extraordinarily special. In many ways, this question was the most challenging, because it was asked in all innocence and deserves a very thoughtful reply. That's also why it is first. There might have been a different answer if it came from an adult.

1. GOD, WHO ARE YOU? WHAT ARE YOU? ARE YOU REAL?

We (the God Administration) like your questions a lot. We will answer first with our own question. What is gravity? We're not asking what it DOES, but what IS it? It is everywhere in the universe, but you cannot see it or touch it. Everything has gravity, even you. It is impossible to remove gravity from a thing without destroying the thing. It is an energy that is part of everything. Some people think of God the same way, as an energy that is part of everything. God is not a person, so don't try to think of God that way.

Some people point to the Bible and remind us that it says there that God made people in God's own image. But that's not true. It is arrogance for someone to think that God made billions of species of animals and plants, but made THEM alone to look like God. No, the truth is that people made God in PEOPLE'S image, because that is as deep as most people can think. They cannot imagine God as nothing and everything at the same time. No, God is not a "Who." God is not a "What." God is real if you believe God is real. God is nothing if you believe God is nothing. There is no right or wrong with God. There is only truth, and the truth is beyond your knowing. The way to live your life is to find what is true FOR you INSIDE you. Do not wait for God to help you or solve your problems. The answers to your questions for God are already in you if you just have the innocence and openness to listen. But go ahead and read the rest of this book anyway.

2. IS GOD A MAN OR A WOMAN, OR SOME OTHER GENDER?

God has no parts you can classify as male or female. Drawings of God with a beard and muscles are ridiculous. Of course, calling God the "Queen of Heaven" is just as silly and just as sexist. God's not a "he" or a "she," and there are no other genders to be. For more on what God is, see the next question.

3. WHAT IS GOD'S FAVORITE COOKIE?

God doesn't actually *eat* food, because, well, what's the point? However, God did invent the five senses: hearing, sight, touch, smell, and taste. God's very proud of coming up with senses for all living things. Taste was the last sense God created, and we did some experiments with things that would be particularly pleasing to the taste buds. We considered this question, and God agreed that any cookie with chocolate in it has to be our favorite.

Speaking of eating, a woman wrote a letter to the *Pittsburgh Post-Gazette* a few years ago saying that same-sex marriages make God sick to his stomach, and we thought, "God has a stomach?" If you're the Supreme Being of the universe and you are everywhere at once, it's not easy getting take-out. But God does eat. God eats time. You know how people say, "Wow, where did the time go?" Well...

Okay, let me get serious. Time is infinite; it stretches out ahead of us forever. But it also stretches out *behind* us forever. In the beginning, there <u>was</u> no beginning, just more time before that. Time passes, but it does not disappear. It's just that we can only see the instant of time that is passing us NOW. (This would be a particularly good place to snap your fingers as you read this.) But time past is still there, and everything that happened in that past is still there, too. And all those events of all time not only <u>feed</u> God, but they <u>become</u> God. They are the reality no longer real in THIS (snap) instant. You cannot see them again, you cannot touch them or hear them again, but you <u>know</u> them. In your mind, they seem real.

14

4. WHAT DO YOU DO ON YOUR DAY OFF, GOD?

We catch up on email. That's "e" as in "ethereal mail."

Okay, I confess. That's just a tongue-in-cheek response. It drives God nuts when I do that. Here's the real reply. "Day" is not a term that has any meaning for God. The Earth is not the only planet in your solar system, which is just one solar system in your galaxy, which is only one galaxy in your universe. And if you think there's only one universe, think again. The word "day" implies both time and light. Measurements of time, as I just said, have no meaning to God. Nor does light and dark. And "day off" implies work. God does not do "work" in the sense that people here think of it; God works in mysterious ways, indeed.

5. WHAT DOES GOD DO FOR FUN? DOES GOD HAVE A HOBBY?

What do you think *you* are? (Just kidding!)

A hobby is something you use to pass the time when you are not engaged in the act of survival. God does not pass the time because God IS time. God is always "on." It is not possible for God to take time off. God did not "rest" on the seventh day or any other day. (See Question 54 about the biblical story of creation.)

When you do something "for fun," you do it because you want to, not because you *have* to. God has no such choice. It would not only be impossible for God to be "off duty" and ready to go have fun; it would be a bad idea. God doesn't have moods (another good thing), so God does not need to unwind or hang out or get loose. God is not just one of the guys hitting the bar after work.

6. WHAT'S A TYPICAL DAY IN THE LIFE OF GOD?

Oh, how we hate to nitpick, but God is not alive and does not have a "day." But perhaps you meant a typical Earth day, and want to know what God is doing then.

God does not actually "do" anything. God is not a thinker or a doer. God is just, well, God. You might as well ask what gravity does on a typical day. (See Question 4 about how God works.)

7. DOES GOD SLEEP?

The ability to sleep is something God considers the greatest gift. (See Question 78, What is God's greatest gift to the living?) Almost every living thing sleeps or has moments of rest. Sleep is a mysterious event that, for people at least, allows the mind to enter realms it cannot otherwise enter. It also bends and distorts time, which is something almost magical. God does not sleep or rest. God is not a person or a living thing, and has no need of sleep or a need to bend time, because God IS time. (See Question 3, What is God's favorite cookie?)

8. DOES GOD AGE?

Yes, but not in the way all temporary things age. Time passes for God as it does for everything, so in a sense, you could say that God ages, or at least has been _through_ the ages. Yet all permanent things – energy and atomic particles, and God – have always existed. They were never "new," so they cannot become the opposite of "new." In general, you would say something ages from its inception. You count your age from the time you were born. We count other things from the time they occurred. We say, for example, that the last Ice Age occurred about 10,000 years ago. Since God has no inception, no point of creation, we cannot give God's age. How old is forever? (See Question 62 about God's existence.)

9. CAN GOD SPEAK EVERY LANGUAGE?

God doesn't "speak" _any_ language. God has no voice. God has no mouth. God cannot hear, yet God is not deaf. God has no ears. God does not listen. "Language" is meaningless to God. God does not use a microphone or loudspeaker. Talking to God is like talking to the air.

10. HOW DOES GOD COMMUNICATE MESSAGES TO MANKIND? TO WHAT EXTENT CAN THE UNDERSTANDING OF MAN COMPREHEND GOD?

God communicates to *human*kind in ways that few, if any, people understand. God does not use words or any language. There are no "messages" that God wants to send to you, and if there were, God would not encode them in some way that would leave any doubt as to their meaning. Certainly, God will never again give a message to just one person and hope that it will be accurately conveyed. (See Questions 38 and 152 about Moses.)

Instead, God communicates in ways that all things, living and non-living, take in – through bursts of energy, some of which are manifested as light waves (which of course also include color), and some of which are sound waves. Do you know why all people like music so much? Because music is the cosmos talking!

Let me take a stab at this comprehension issue. Try to stay with me here, because it's complicated. No *physical* thing can be in two places at the same time, so for God to be everywhere, either God is not a physical thing OR the cosmos is all one place. The cosmos is infinite, that is, it has no end point. If it is one piece, then God must be infinite, too, in order to be everywhere at once. That would mean God is the cosmos, and that's what some people believe. But God and the cosmos are *not* the same thing. The cosmos has fewer dimensions.

Time is the only infinite that is everywhere at once. Let me repeat that. Time is the only infinite that is everywhere at once. It is impossible to define time in words. (Go ahead… try. All the definitions that people come up with include words like "period," "past," "future," and "duration," which don't really tell you what time IS.) Time is God, and yes, it is everywhere at once. It exists

18

even in the vast voids of space. It is the same moment in time everywhere in the cosmos. Most intelligent-life forms in the universe have a concept of God similar to the popular concepts here on Earth. Only a few life forms truly understand what time is, and they do not worship it.

11. HOW CAN WE CONTACT GOD?

Pick up your phone and hit the "infinity" button. Yours doesn't have one? I'd let you use my cell phone, but the roaming charges would kill me. Sorry.

12. WHEN CAN I MEET YOU, GOD?

God wants to know if you are single and, if so, where you'd like to go on your first date.

Actually, that wasn't God's answer. That was God's humble press secretary making a bad joke. You cannot "meet" God, but you experience God every moment of your life, even when you are asleep.

13. WHY IS THERE SO MUCH CONFUSION ABOUT GOD'S EXISTENCE?

God likes it that way. Suppose there was no confusion. Suppose all the truths about God and the universe were revealed to everyone, or anyone, for that matter. Life would be joyless and gray. People would have nothing left to hope for because they would know too much. Confusion is basically good, although it has led to some of the nastier events of history, too.

Those people who claim to understand God and to have attained "enlightenment," whatever that is, have barely scratched the surface.

14. AS AN AGNOSTIC, I CANNOT REALLY KNOW IF GOD EXISTS. DOES GOD HAVE A SIMILAR PROBLEM? GOD, ARE YOU SURE THAT YOU ARE GOD? IS THERE ONLY ONE OF YOU?

There is no concept of "one" for God. We already said there is no "day" and no "on" or "off." Numbers are also meaningless when you are infinite. You cannot divide by zero, and you cannot divide the infinite. If God is in every _thing_, God cannot also be just ONE thing. To be everyplace is to be no _single_ place. Therefore, one infinite God is, from a practical standpoint, exactly the same as no God, which is just the way God likes it.

That is why God created atheists, for in their denial of God, they come closer to God than anyone. The atheist cannot prove the nonexistence of God. That concept is, by definition, impossible. You cannot prove a negative. So, the atheist accepts _on faith_ that God does not exist, because such a thing as God is beyond comprehension. The believer, on the other hand, cannot prove that God DOES exist, and so they, too, use faith to replace what reason alone cannot fathom. Only the agnostic has no faith, for as soon as they begin to lean in one direction, their reason pulls them back in the other direction. Agnostics are the magnetic levitators of truth. It is all beyond the possibility of humans ever to know or understand. One God, many gods, no gods; it is all the same.

The important thing to remember is that you should never confuse faith and hope with fact. Just because you believe with all your heart that something is "true" does not _necessarily_ make it so.

15. WHY ISN'T LIFE GETTING ANY BETTER? WHY COULDN'T YOU HAVE MADE THINGS A LITTLE BIT EASIER ON ALL OF US DOWN HERE? WHY DISEASE? WHY HATE? WHY RAPE AND MURDER AND LYING AND MOSQUITOES AND ROTTEN FRUIT AND FLOODS AND FAMINE? DO YOU REALLY LOVE US? WHY DID YOU CREATE US? AND IF YOU CAN'T ANSWER THESE QUESTIONS, IF I CAN NEVER KNOW THE ANSWERS, THEN WHY DID YOU MAKE ME CAPABLE OF ASKING THEM? *

If you had all the answers, would you be satisfied? Would you feel comforted? Isn't there some comfort in being able to ask and ponder and *not* knowing all the answers? If there were one answer, would everyone on Earth accept it, or would it become just another source of division and anger? Many people may say they truly want to know all the answers, to know the mysteries that abound, but most of these people also believe they already know the answers and are just looking for confirmation of their faith. What if the answers did not match their faith? Would they reject their faith? Or would they reject the answers? History suggests people would reject the answers and keep the blind faith, because it comforts them.

Since not everyone has the same answers and the same faith, there would be billions of people instantly shaken if God gave you the truth. (Isn't this reminiscent of Jack Nicholson's line in "A Few Good Men?" He said, "The truth? You can't handle the truth." How right he was!) If God dispelled all the mysteries of life, the result would be *more* chaos, not less.

---

* All questions taken from "Faxes to God" by Dr. Joyce Starr are indicated by an asterisk.

16. IS GOD OMNISCIENT AND OMNIPOTENT? IF SO, THEN WHY DO PEOPLE HAVE TO SUFFER? IF THE ANSWER IS NO, THEN WHY DO PEOPLE BELIEVE GOD IS? EITHER WAY, DOES IT MATTER?

The answer depends on what you mean by "omniscient" and "omnipotent." If you mean that God knows everything and has the power to control everything, the answer is no.

God does not know everything. In fact, God does not really "know" *any*thing, not the way a person knows things. Remember, God is not a person. God does not have a mind and a memory. God does not *see* things, either. God is present in all things, but feels nothing.

Do people suffer? Don't blame God if you do. You were not created to suffer. That would imply you were created for a purpose, and you were not. You were merely created to exist, not to serve some higher purpose that you have yet to discern. Don't waste time even trying to figure it out. Thousands of generations of Earth people have been born and lived and died without knowing their purpose. Were their lives wasted by not knowing? Of course not! The reason you do not know your purpose is that there is no purpose to know. (See Question 79, What is the meaning of life?) If God made you to suffer, it would have to be for a reason, and since there is no such reason, you can assume that God does not control your suffering. Or your joy. Or anything else in your life. You have the power to end your own suffering, or at least some of it. God gives you freedom, and some choose to squander it on seeking slavery and calling it "belief." You're darned right it matters!

17. Jeremiah, I have a follow-up question. IS GOD ALL GOOD?

God is not "good" the way a person or the weather or a sandwich is good. God cannot be any of the values you use to compare people, and that's a good thing.

The word "good" is a relative term. For something to be good, there must also be a way for it to be *bad*. Relative qualities don't apply to God. God is just God, neither good nor bad. If God COULD be good or bad, you Earth people would be in big trouble, because you'd never know what's coming, what the rules are. God could be capricious, which would NOT be a good thing. (See Question 210 about good and evil, and Question 171, How does a good God account for the evil in the world?)

Nothing God does is bad at its moment of creation or change. But not every creation or change works out well. God does not control how things turn out, so you could say that God is never bad, but that is not exactly the same as saying God is all good.

18. DO YOU FEEL PEOPLE EXPECT TOO MUCH OF GOD?

No, not really. What does it hurt for them to expect? Expecting and hoping are very close, and hope is a good thing. What frosts our comet tails is a person who demands too much and gets angry when nothing happens. Someone once said, "God answers every prayer, but sometimes the answer is No." (See Question 160, Does God listen to prayers?)

23

19. WHAT DOES GOD THINK OF ATHEISTS?
God doesn't believe in atheists. Next question.

Oh, okay, you want more of an answer. Here goes:

It is very sobering to think that all of a sudden at some point you simply will cease to exist in any form. How can somebody possibly take that information in and process the idea that they simply will not exist anymore? So, of course, anybody who says you're going to disappear completely forever – there will be no soul, there will be no heaven – is saying something that's really frightening, and nobody wants to hear that. Atheists need to recognize that.

The fact that they're correct about some things shouldn't make them so damn smug.

Did I forget to mention at Question 16 that I was just kidding about God creating atheists? Oh, you figured that out? Good.

20. IS IT LONELY BEING THE ONLY GOD?

Ah, you are making several assumptions here about the nature of God. First, you are assuming that God has emotions like loneliness. Second, you are assuming that there is only one God. Third, you imply that if there is just one God, then nothing besides another God could prevent loneliness.

Let's consider each of these assumptions. As it turns out, there is only one God, but older religions that considered many gods were not that far off the mark. They simply misunderstood what a god is. The fact that they saw a god in each aspect of life and nature is correct, except that they did not realize that all things in which the work of God is present are, in fact, the same God. Their mistake was in believing that God controls the physical and spiritual world, and so they had gods of the seas and of thunder, of war and of love. But God, being nothing more (or less) than time, is simply the force that set all these things in motion at their origin, and does not control them at all. Since there can be only one point of creation, there can be only one God.

God does not feel emotions, and that's a good thing. Imagine if God could feel lonely. With no other gods to break up the solitude, where would God turn for companionship? Hey, I'm just a humble press secretary. *I'm* not going to try to fill THOSE big shoes! What would be the consequences if the creator of the universe got downcast? Not only that, but what would you do to try to lighten the mood? Play Twister®? And just think how good God would be at, say, Scrabble®! "Hey, God, THAT'S not a word!" "It *is* on the planet Blorph!" Who in their right mind would want to try to be a companion to God? Talk about a no-win situation.

21. HOW DID GOD COME TO BE GOD? WHERE DID GOD COME FROM?

This question may be the most difficult of all to answer, because there is no way to express God in terms Earthlings can understand. God does not come from anything or anywhere.

People want to think of everything in terms that relate to their own experience. Every person you know was created. You may have created some people yourself. You will not meet every human contemporary of yours, but you will encounter as many as several million during your lifetime. Some people you like, some you don't like, and most you never get to know at all. They are fellow passengers on the bus or plane, people who pass you on the sidewalk, other spectators at the game or concert or movie, or celebrities you see repeatedly but never get to know. So, naturally, many of you think of God as just another contemporary, just another "fellow traveler" on this shiny bright planet. Unfortunately, that puts you off the track completely.

Many people get hung up on the conundrum that if God did all the creating, then what created God? You will get nowhere thinking like that! It's an impossible riddle to solve. It's not like there was some ethereal Board of Directors that checked résumés and appointed the top candidate. God was always there. Even God does not know what created God. There is no point even thinking about it. So many people spend so much precious time contemplating the nature of God and the origin of the cosmos. You can never know more than God knows, or even half as much as God knows. Accept that some things will never be known. Read the question after next regarding God's "biography."

22. WHO IS GOD'S MOTHER?

There is no beginning or end to God. God has no mother, nothing that created God. There is no "before" to God. Anyway, if you think raising *teen*agers is tough, can you imagine being God's mother? "Where are you going, God?" "Out." "You can't go out. You're everywhere." It wouldn't work.

23. CAN YOU GIVE US A BIOGRAPHY OF GOD?

God is, was, and always will be. That kind of sums it up.

From the other answers in this press conference, you can infer a "biography" of God. But remember that God is not living, and the word "biography" comes from the Greek "bios" meaning "life. For Earth people, it is easier to understand what God is <u>not</u> than to understand what God is. God is omnipresent, but not omnipotent. God is not human or emotional or calculating. God creates everything and controls nothing. God is in every place and in no *one* place. God is every language, yet does not communicate in any of them. God is zero and God is one, total darkness and blinding light.

The big difference between God and everything else is that nothing about God is pure chance and everything else *is*. God is time. Time is a constant everywhere in the cosmos. Time always was and always will be, and so there is no opportunity for time to be subject to the whims of chance. The difference between one moment in time and the next is represented by change. All change is pure chance. There is no way to know or control the nearly infinite changes that occur in the cosmos at each moment's passing.

27

24. IF GOD IS WITHOUT ATTRIBUTES, HOW ARE OUR OBJECTIFYING MINDS SUPPOSED TO KNOW GOD?

You're NOT supposed to know God. If you want to *try* to understand God, that's your business, but don't expect your search to matter to God. God doesn't want to be known or worshipped. Don't feel badly if you haven't spent your life trying to comprehend God. The important thing is not what intellectual plane you have achieved, but whether you have lived your life well. (See Question 41, Why are you invisible?)

25. IS THERE ALWAYS THE SAME GOD? CAN SOMEONE NEW BECOME GOD?

God is God. There is no beginning or end to the job. God cannot retire or change into something other than God. There will never be a different God or an additional God. God does not have interns or apprentices. Would YOU want to be God? The hours suck, there's no pay, no benefits, and no time off, EVER. Maybe God should join a union.

26. WHO OR WHAT CAN REPLACE GOD?

Nothing. God is irreplaceable. (See Question 23 about God's biography, and the previous question.) God cannot die or wear out, and anyway, the warranty on God expired eons ago.

27. WHERE DID GOD DWELL BEFORE THE BIRTH OF THE UNIVERSE?

Before the birth of *this* universe there was another universe that was born and grew old and died, and another universe before that. The Bible states there was a "void," but there was never a total void. There always was the same amount of "stuff" as there is now, but it reshapes itself and regenerates itself again and again and again, and will do so forever. And when God says "forever," it's not like when someone says they'll love you forever. God really means *forever*.

The interesting thing about the concept of infinity is that you Earth people can imagine it going forward, but not going backward. People say, okay, now that matter and energy exist, of course they will exist forever and ever, even if this universe someday implodes and another Big Bang comes along. But Earthlings – and most intelligent beings elsewhere in the cosmos – cannot grasp the same concept looking into the past. You feel like there just *had to* be a start to it all, and that before that start, there was so much nothing that even *time* didn't exist, but just empty space and no matter.

See, *that's* where you lose it. You think that time can't exist if there are no events. It's the old "tree falls in the woods" puzzle. How can there be time if there is nothing against which to measure time? Einstein and others have argued that time and space are four dimensional, and that they rely on each other to exist. That's not even *close*. God IS time. If nothing else existed, there would still be time. In other words, even nothing is something. Yet there has never been nothing, never been more than an instant when all matter and energy condensed to almost nothing and then exploded again into a whole new cosmos. And here's the *really* hard part to conceive – when all matter and energy in the universe contracts, there

29

is still something that fills the void left by the shrinking universe, and there is still something out beyond all the matter that has condensed. It is another entire cosmos, and beyond that another. There is no beginning or end to space. There is no beginning or end to time. There is no beginning or end to God. Where did God dwell before? There is no "before" to God.

28. WHERE DOES GOD LIVE NOW? DOES HE HAVE A WIFE?

God does not "live" the way you think of life. All living things share certain characteristics, and almost none of these pertain to God's existence. God does not breathe, for example, or take in nourishment, or expel waste. God does not experience the universe in the same way as people do, using just five senses. And God does not feel emotion as some intelligent life forms do.

Finally, God has no gender. Therefore, God does not have a "wife" or a "husband." Can you imagine being Mrs. God? If you think HUMAN spouses are hard to please... Oh, man.

29. WHO IS GOD'S GOD? WHO DOES GOD ANSWER TO?

Interesting concept, and very human in its premise. And, of course, it's natural in human terms to think, "If God created everything, who or what created God?" (See Question 21, How did you come to be God?)

As we point out in Question 14 about agnostics, there is really no difference whether you think in terms of no God, one God, or many gods. You still end up in the same place, and a good, productive life still depends on what you do, not some external force. The ancient civilizations that postulated many gods – the Greeks, Romans, Egyptians, and Norsemen – all presumed that the gods were not equal, that one must be the God of all gods. (See Question 129 about God's support staff.) They were correct in their vision that God was present in all things, but wrong in thinking there is any kind of inequality in the cosmos. To God, a rock, a person, and oxygen are all the same. None is more or less important than the others.

You cannot take anything away from infinity and still have infinity. God, being everything, leaves no room for some *other* thing that is *not* God. If there were anything in the cosmos that were not God, that one thing, no matter how small or seemingly insignificant, would have dominion over God. That concept is impossible. And so, God does not "answer" to anyone or anything. All is God; God is all. God always was; God always will be. Nothing created God. God created nothing. I just *hate* trying to explain this to Earth people.

30. CAN GOD PROCRASTINATE?

Can we get back to you on that?

31. HOW SHOULD WE WORSHIP GOD?

We on God's staff do not understand why people worship God. That is not what God wants. If you really want to honor God, you will do so by respecting all other people, all living things, and the planet God has created for you. Too many people worship GOD while desecrating and destroying God's work.

It's good to show appreciation and gratitude for one's life, but it is not productive to worship God for doing what God does naturally. The best missionaries are those who let their appreciation show through the work they do, not through trying to talk about God. God does not want or need more worshippers, but God would prefer that more people become shepherds for the Earth and for unfortunate people and animals on the Earth.

32. SOME PEOPLE SAY THAT GOD IS LOVE. IS THAT TRUE?

God *created* love, but God is not love, nor does God feel love. Love is a very human emotion, and God is not human. God does not love you. God does not hate you, either. God is pretty indifferent to all creation. Take it from me, that's not a bad thing. If God were not neutral about objects in the cosmos and the things on those objects – things like *you*, for instance – there probably wouldn't even be an Earth.

33. IT IS SAID, "CLEANLINESS IS NEXT TO GODLINESS." IS *THIS* TRUE?

What rubbish (pun intended)! Surely it was an exasperated mother who first uttered these words. God does not care if you or your children are "clean." The concept has no meaning to God. God is not obsessive-compulsive, like some crazed mother-in-law who seeks to prove that her son's wife is not the housekeeper she ought to be. You get no points with God for washing behind your ears and scrubbing your fingernails. Who do you think created dirt in the first place?

34. SINCE GOD IS SO POWERFUL AND MAGNIFICENT, WHY WOULD GOD STOOP TO DESTROY AN INSIGNIFICANT INDIVIDUAL JUST BECAUSE SHE DOESN'T BELIEVE IN GOD? AND, IF GOD IS A LOVING GOD, WHY WOULD GOD MAKE PEOPLE BURN IN HELL FOR ETERNITY?

What an unusual question! Is this the Almighty version of the "When did you stop beating your wife" trap?

We saw a sign outside a church recently that said, "You have to believe to receive." We were not amused by this message of intolerance, and we found it insulting to God[1]. It implies that God rewards people based on their beliefs, not their actions. It says that God needs your praise and worship, or you cannot receive whatever these closed-minded people think God hands out. It says that no matter how kind you are, no matter what good things you do with your life, you are doomed if you do not believe in the God they are promoting. What rubbish! Do they really think God is that petty, that God has no interest in part of God's creations just because of what that creation *thinks?* No wonder so many people think so little of God, with this kind of fuzzy proselytizing.

God does not "stoop." God does not "destroy." God has no ability to destroy, although God did plant the means for destruction in all of nature.

No person is "insignificant," or at least, no less significant than anyone else, unless you count paparazzi. If a person is "destroyed" because of whatever she believes, blame it on other people who think they know God's will

---

[1] God, not having emotions, cannot feel insults, but something can still be insulting in nature. Just because a person does not hear an abusive comment about them does not mean the comment was not abusive.

and have given themselves the authority to act on this false knowledge.

As for burning in hell for eternity (or even for a few minutes), see Question 117, Is there a place called hell?

35. DOES GOD DEMAND OR RESPOND TO SACRIFICES?

Why would God create things and then demand that those things be destroyed? How did anyone come up with the idea that destruction would please God? When people or animals die, they do not become "angels" who then keep company with God or do God's "work" (see Question 4, What do you do on your day off?), as is the belief popular with so many. So, what benefit could God derive from their deliberate death? Why would this kind of evil appease God? In fact, God does not *need* appeasing. God is not some flamboyant hotel manager who decides to make your life miserable and hopes you'll slip him a little something on the side. God's only reaction to sacrifice is that it shows how little Earth people understand the universe.

36. HOW DID GOD EVER GET THE REPUTATION OF BEING PERFECT, ALL-WISE, ALL-KNOWING? GOD IS SUPPOSED TO BE PERFECT, TO KNOW EVERYTHING. BUT THEN, OUT OF THIS PERFECTION, GOD CREATES AN IMPERFECT UNIVERSE – ESPECIALLY OUR LITTLE SPECK OF DUST, EARTH. WHY DIDN'T GOD LEAVE WELL ENOUGH ALONE?

God is not all-wise OR all-knowing, and so has no idea how that rumor started. There is a common misconception that God knows everything about everything and just parcels it out a little at a time, or prevents you Earth people from learning "the truth." (See Question 48 about quantum mechanics.)

Leave well enough alone? God did not create the Earth to be what it is. God IS creation, and all that exists follows its own path, not some predestined fate decreed by God. Most universes exist for a few seconds and then collapse. A few, like yours, last much, much longer. The forces that interact in any universe are random and unplanned. It is precisely BECAUSE God leaves well enough alone that you exist at all!

37. IF THERE IS BOTH MATTER AND ANTI-
MATTER, THEN IS THERE ALSO GOD AND ANTI-
GOD? IN OTHER WORDS, IS THERE A DEVIL, A
SATAN THAT CREATES AND CONTROLS ALL THE
BAD THINGS IN THE UNIVERSE?

Satan exists only in myths and stories, and in the
minds of some people, good and bad. There is no devil, no
hell, no angel banished from God's heaven. Indeed, there
are no angels at all and there's no heaven full of souls.

People have found Satan a useful scapegoat for
centuries. "The devil made me do," said Flip Wilson, and
everyone knew it was a joke. Because the devil never made
anyone do anything. There is no cunning, evil, human-like
devil any more than there is a wise, merciful, human-like
God. The flowing-beard, rippling-muscles image of God is
a fanciful creation of humans, and so is the sharp-horned,
red-skinned image of Satan. There is no such God, and
there is no anti-God of any kind.

38. THERE ARE PEOPLE WHO CLAIM GOD HAS SPOKEN WITH THEM, OR APPEARED TO THEM IN A VISION, OR GUIDED THEIR HAND AS THEY WROTE. HAS GOD DONE THOSE THINGS?

Apparently these people have never read Freud or Jung. It bears repeating: God does not intervene in human life, or any other creation. Even allowing this Press Conference is something God hesitated to do, because it could be considered an intervention. Some of us feel that it is, and cautioned against publishing these answers. As you can see, we lost.

The *only* other time God stepped in was when God handed Moses the Seven Commandments (see Question 152 on the Ten Commandments). And in retrospect, God thinks that was a mistake.

Other than that, God has never "spoken" to any human, or planted visions in their minds while they sleep (which would be one heck of a trick, wouldn't it?), or made them write or say something that their own brain did not create. Those people who claim otherwise are either lying to you or to themselves. To be kind, we will suggest simply that they are not familiar with the power of their own subconscious. (See Question 209 about George Bush and Osama bin Laden.)

39. IS IT JUST A COINCIDENCE THAT "GOD" IS "DOG" SPELLED BACKWARDS?

Yes. It's also just coincidence that "devil" spelled backwards is "lived."

40. WHAT DOES GOD LOOK LIKE?

What does time look like, or gravity, or a sigh? God has no appearance of any kind. Many artists try to depict God as beams of light, but that is a feeble and inaccurate attempt. God is as much darkness as light, as much silence as sound. The worst depictions show God as a person, almost always a man. That is not only wrong, it's destructive, for it causes people to think of God as male. Animals and other beings don't have that misconception, and so enjoy greater freedom. Because people cannot see God, some people think of God as invisible.

41. WHY IS GOD INVISIBLE? *

God is not invisible. You simply don't know what to look for because you've probably been told that God looks like an old man who still likes to work out at the gym. If you go searching for _that_ God, you'll be disappointed your whole life. Unless you have a "thing" for buff old guys who _think_ they're God.

In one sense, though, God _is_ invisible. You will never be able to look at one thing and see all of God. God hides in plain sight. God is time and time is change, and those are things you cannot see directly. Instead, you can see the _result_ of God in all creation and especially in watching the way things change. Study an old person's face or hands. Watch a butterfly flaps its wings. Catch the snow on your tongue. Throw a leaf into the wind. Bury a rock in the sand. In all these things, God is visible.

42. I'd like to ask a follow-up question. CAN GOD TAKE ON HUMAN FORM AND APPEAR AMONG US? HAS GOD EVER DONE THAT?

Apparently, you have seen too many Las Vegas magic shows or too many cheesy Hollywood movies. God is not some kind of circus performer or illusionist. God has no need to resort to cheap, melodramatic theatrical tricks. And even if God *could* take on another form, what makes you think that God would want to appear human? Why not a frog or an eagle or a fungus?

This notion that God might temporarily become a person seems to come from Earth people's desire to think of God as a benevolent father-figure, someone whose primary wish is to "make things right" for people led astray. You would think that the most important thing to God is to make sure that some poor clod doesn't marry the wrong girl, or that the stuck-up cheerleader finally discovers what brings *true* happiness. Oh and by the way, pay no attention to all those millions of starving people or war orphans or cancer patients. What God must really want is a sappy musical score playing while God plays "Touched by an Angel" for some suburbanite with low self-esteem.

God is not coming to Earth. God is not your father. God is not your mother. God does not care about any one person more than any other person. And God is _not_ "the man upstairs." Please stop saying that! It makes God sound like a boarder who could come galumphing down the steps any minute, demanding more hot water and some clean sheets.

Look at it another way. God has been around forever. People have been around less than a million years. Do you think God sat around moping for all those billions of eons until God got the big idea to create people? Do you think people are just some kind of diversion or amusement for God? One person lives about 120 years at most. One star lasts about 100 billion years. So if God could pick favorite creations, which do you think, based on the evidence, God would care more about? Here's a hint: "You are the weakest link. Goodbye."

43. GOD, WHY NOT REVEAL YOURSELF IN SOME FORM TO THE MODERN WORLD IN ORDER TO STOP THE CURRENT MAYHEM?

What makes you think God has not been revealed? God is visible in so many things (see the previous three questions). And yet, the mayhem continues. That should tell you something.

44. WHERE IS THE GODDESS? WE HAVE "ONE NATION UNDER GOD," AND "IN GOD WE TRUST." I WOULD THINK THE GODDESS WOULD BE PRETTY UPSET BY NOW FOR NOT GETTING HER FAIR SHARE OF WORSHIP.

Oh, my. If God could snicker, this question would do it. You've made the common mistake of assuming that God is a male term. Certainly, that's how most people in the world use the term, believing that God equals power and power equals male. But God also equals creation and creation equals female. God has no gender. Depictions of God as a man are misleading and destructive. (See Question 2 about God's gender and Question 40 about God's appearance.)

A Press Conference with God

III. CREATION
Or, 'SCUSE ME WHILE I KISS THE SKY

At the heart of all the theological searching of humanity is the central question, "Where did we come from?" People want to know the story of their own creation. They hope it will help tell them why they are "here," which really means why they exist at all. Most people think of God as the creator, whether they anthropomorphize God (that is, imagine God as having human or lifelike qualities), or simply think of God AS creation itself. One way or another, "God" represents that which created everything we see, touch, think, and feel. Of course, the next issue after finding out about our own creation is finding out what *else* got created that we don't experience ourselves.

45. EVOLUTION OR CREATION?

The answer should be obvious to everyone. Is the universe the same today as it was even one minute ago? Every change in one thing ultimately changes all other things, even in minute ways. A ship cutting through the water creates ripples that move across entire oceans. These ripples push droplets into the air, some of which are carried on winds and dropped on parched soil or into reservoirs. The person who drinks this drop is changed by it, and each small action they take changes other people and the environment. All is part of the interconnected web of existence.

Suppose God DID create Earth's people and all the beasts and plants exactly as you know them now. Suppose nothing that exists today evolved from something else. That would mean that God thinks the world is perfect just this way. Let me tell you, anyone who thinks this is the best God could do is crazy. OF COURSE there is evolution. God pushes the "start" button, and then we watch to see what something can do to improve itself. Haven't you done things to improve yourself? You are living proof of evolution.

The very diversity that you see on Earth is further proof. The differences between people are not just cultural. There are physical differences, ways in which bodies have adapted to the different environments of Earth. You humans are evolving constantly. Look at how much taller people are becoming. *That's* evolution. Children are becoming smarter at a younger age. In the future, your children may be born knowing how to do things that today they learn at three or four.

How can anyone deny the existence of evolution, its role in all of nature? Just look at AIDS and SARS, two diseases that did not exist until recently. These viruses evolved, and there will be hundreds more such viruses, and humans' bodies will adapt to fight them off. It will be this way forever. If bugs can evolve, why not people?

On the other hand, some people look at evolution and see it as intelligent design. They miss the mark, too. For example, strong winds come and prune the weak and dying branches from a tree, leaving it stronger despite the destruction. Yet all such phenomena are simply coincidence. Nature does not deliberately, with cunning and forethought, protect itself. God does not control the natural world. It functions just fine without help, thank you.

This concept of "intelligent design" is the most preposterous and insulting idea you humans have yet to concoct. Look at the chaos that is your world. We don't mean just what you Earthlings do to each other, but every aspect of your planet. If this place – as spectacular as it sometimes can be – is what "intelligence" wrought, then you must have a pretty low opinion of God's abilities.

Finally, you must recognize that "evolution" refers to the non-physical world as well. Human intellect and philosophy and ideas and concepts of God have changed continuously. The bodies of Third Millennium people (i.e. YOU) are nearly the same, with some obvious changes, as people from 4000 years ago, but you cannot equate people today with people then because your *thoughts* are so different.

46. IN THE POEM "TREES," JOYCE KILMER WROTE, "ONLY GOD CAN MAKE A TREE." IS THAT TRUE?

No, it's not.

Only God can make the primordial soup from which a tree may ultimately develop, given the right planetary conditions, but even God does not make an individual tree or design a species of tree.

So, the question could then be, what else or who else could make a tree? Clearly, no being on Earth has *yet* made a tree, but you have come close. Earth people have created new species of trees and other plants, and even new species of animals, through careful breeding of organisms that already exist. The next step is for Earth people to create a living thing out of non-living ingredients. There is no way to predict whether that will ever occur, but it HAS occurred on other planets. Earthlings show signs of having the intelligence to figure out how to "make a tree." Hopefully, that will not happen any time soon, for if it were to occur on today's Earth the "creator" would certainly be tortured and killed by people too superstitious or too fixed in their own beliefs to allow such a thing. Just look at your debate about cloning. (See Question 227, Does God condone cloning?)

47. PEOPLE SAY EVERY DAY IS A GIFT FROM GOD. IS IT?

That you have life is the gift from God. What you do with it is your gift to yourself. Be careful how you unwrap it.

48. IS QUANTUM MECHANICS RECONCILABLE WITH RELATIVITY, AND IS STRING THEORY THE MECHANISM?

Is this question going to be on the final? It's kind of charming that you think God would know this stuff, and that if God DID know, that God would tell *you*. Your question reflects the common misconception that God knows everything about everything and just parcels it out a little at a time, or prevents Earth people from learning "the truth." That, as we say, is "comet droppings."

Here is a partial list of things that God is not:
- A mind reader
- A scientist
- A psychologist
- An artist
- A mathematician
- A psychic
- An oddsmaker
- A baseball player, football player, hockey player, golfer, tennis player, soccer player, or track and field star
- Jewish, Catholic, Muslim, Buddhist, Hindu, Protestant, Mormon, or Freethinker
- Your pal
- Your enemy
- An economist
- A biologist
- A landscaper
- A doctor
- A lawyer
- And last, but not least, God is not a comedian

Suppose, for a moment, that God DOES know the answer to this question and to all other questions about

47

science. Suppose it were true, as some Earth people believe, that God made everything according to some design, and that God even made the design itself, using very complex and sophisticated mechanisms like string theory. What would that say about God that is not insulting?

Here's what we mean. If God knows what causes every disease, if God knows how to combine DNA to produce different life forms and change life, if God, in fact, knows everything about everything, then why would God allow thousands of generations of people to suffer without cures for diseases and without adequate food and with all the other evils that you are just now learning how to eliminate? What kind of God would deliberately withhold valuable information from you? What kind of God would force you to discover scientific truths a little bit at a time? The answer is that NO God would do that. NO God would make something like Earthlings and then let them suffer and die for lack of something God knows but won't divulge. And that simple fact is all you need to prove that God is not controlling your destiny.

49. ONE OF THE GOD'S BILLBOARD "QUOTES FROM GOD" SAYS, "BIG BANG THEORY. YOU'VE GOT TO BE KIDDING." WHAT ABOUT THE "BIG BANG" THEORY? IS IT WRONG?

What confuses God is that people who claim to believe in the God of the Bible would reject the Big Bang Theory. They really ought to embrace it, because it is EXACTLY what is described in Genesis. If God made everything in the manner that Genesis describes, then all creation emanated from a single point, and I'd call that a pretty Big Bang.

On the other hand, Genesis is not a reliable source of historical or geological fact. It didn't take six days for God to create your universe. (See Question 54 about the biblical story of creation.) It took milliseconds, at least for the creation part. Then it took millions of years for things to settle down and different forms of life to begin from the primordial soup. (See Question 212, What about original sin?)

50. WHY DOES ANYTHING EXIST?

What a question! Drop the first word, and you have an even *more* intriguing question. If nothing existed, how would you know?

51. WHY DO MOSQUITOES EXIST?

Funny – mosquitoes want to know the same thing about people.

Nasty things exist for the same reason that all other things exist. Mosquitoes and cockroaches and viruses and Rush Limbaugh all evolved from the primordial ooze, though clearly the first three have evolved farther. (See Question 15, Why isn't life getting any better?)

52. WHAT ARE GOD'S GREATEST CREATIONS?

God did not actually *create* anything, at least not in the say-an-incantation-and-wave-a-magic-wand kind of way. If God had to pick the greatest stuff in which God exists, God would pick water, Velcro®, DNA, proteins, and the human brain, the last of which is both best AND worst. That's God's list. My personal favorite is the whole matter-into-energy thing. That is so cool.

53. WHAT WAS GOD'S GREATEST FAILURE OR DISAPPOINTMENT?

Microsoft Windows® has never quite worked out as well as we expected.

54. THE BIBLE SAYS GOD CREATED THE WORLD IN SIX DAYS. WHAT'S THE REAL STORY?

Let's talk first about what the Bible *doesn't* say. There's nothing about extinctions, mistakes, and outright failures, but they all occurred. In fact, more than 99 percent of all species ever to exist on Earth have disappeared. The "real story" is that creation just *is*. It's not something that stops at some point. Your planet is never the same place two of your days in a row. It is a living thing. Every day, a new species creates itself using evolution as its key. Every day, another species goes *poof*! Every day, a mountain moves, a glacier melts or is expanded. Every day, water is carried from one spot to another by clouds.

All the matter and energy in the cosmos has always existed and will always exist. Nothing can be created from nothing. The great thing about God is that God IS the nothing and the everything. Why does my jaw always hurt when I tell people that?

Even before your universe came into being, all the components of your universe − every atom − were part of something else. Your Sun, your Earth, your Moon, and everything on them have changed and continue to change. Remember that God is time, and time is change. The complete nature of the things on Earth, both living and non-living, is always in flux.

Six days? Hardly. The billions of years of your universe are to God as six days of your life are to you. (See Question 68 about whether God regrets making humans.)

Now, you've opened up a related subject of concern, which is the matter of what supposedly happened next. You know, where your Bible says, "On the Seventh Day God rested." If you ever went looking for a statement that proves the Bible cannot possibly be the actual Word of God, this is the one. Here's the headline why:

God Doesn't Need to Rest

Can it get much plainer than that? God is not a person. God doesn't get worn out and just put God's Size-Infinity shoes up on God's cosmological hassock and chill out. You've really got to stop picturing God as some sort of Merlin-type wizard who waves his (it's never "her," is it?) arms and conjures things up out of nothing. God is not the ultimate illusionist or alchemist. You can't wear God out.

So, what did God do next? Okay, if you have to ask, you weren't paying close attention at the beginning of this answer. There is no "next." Creation is always happening; it never ends, because time never ends. As soon as one universe collapses and dies, with absolutely no lapse between them, a new universe is born. The black hole reverses pull of all matter (dark and otherwise) into itself, and suddenly explodes it all out, creating a new universe. Time can never end; change is ever infinite. So it's a complete syllogism: God is time; time can never end, and God must exist in every change. To say that God rested is to say that time stood still. As if!

55. IS THE UNIVERSE EXPANDING OR CONTRACTING, AND WHAT HAPPENS TO US?

Your universe is still expanding. Other universes are contracting. See the next two questions for more on this subject.

As to what happens to you, it depends on whether you are looking for a short-term or a long-term prediction. Since your question is about how the universe changes, it appears you are taking a long-term view. In that case, keep reading for the answer. In the short term, while your solar system and your universe remain intact, the future is a lot less clear. Based on a lot of factors, such as your dwindling oil reserves, pollution, climate changes, religious differences, political instability, and the Cannes Film Festival, it would appear you are in deep doo-doo.

56. IS THERE SUCH A THING AS A PARALLEL UNIVERSE?

Not really, although that might help explain why Pat Buchanan still wins votes.

Other universes, yes. Parallel, not exactly.

The other universes exist around (and next to) this universe. Together, all the universes form the cosmos. There are an infinite number of universes. Your scientists recently have been puzzled by the fact that objects flying through this universe are *accelerating*, which would seem illogical if your Big Bang theory is correct.

But it's not illogical at all. The scientists have failed to account for the gravitational effect of contiguous universes. Why can't they see these other universes? Just as black holes in this universe are so dense that not even light can escape, the internal gravity of one universe prevents its light from escaping into the next universe. Even if it were possible to stand at the very edge of this universe, you would not be able to see the next universe a millimeter away.

I see you have a follow-up question?

57. Yes, I do. SO, WE CAN NEVER DO MORE THAN SPECULATE ABOUT OTHER UNIVERSES?

Exactly right. You can theorize they exist right now. You can also theorize that some universes no longer exist, and some are yet to be created, but you can never prove or disprove the theory.

The complete nature of the universe is beyond the capacity of the human mind as currently evolved, so people should stop worrying about it. You cannot know the unknowable. By definition, any prior universe that ended in the Big Bang really ENDED. It left no trace of itself for your or your descendants to discover.

Someday, at a time so distant it is unimaginable to you Earth people, your universe will collapse upon itself and be reborn in a new cataclysm. A new universe, not identical to yours, will come into being. At the same instant, all space and time within your universe will end and be restarted in a new universe.

So, if you believe that there will be or *could* be a new universe after yours dies, isn't it arrogant to think that YOUR universe was the first that ever existed? And if it's not the first, why should it be the second, or the hundredth, or the millionth in the line of an infinite number of universes that have been created and existed and died in more or less the same fashion?

You also must realize, if you insist on pondering such things, that not all universes are created equal. Some barely survive even the lifetime of one Earth person. Survival depends upon the rate of expansion and the status of proximate *other* universes.

Why do you think that a universe cannot evolve in the same manner as things *within* the universe evolve? In the same way you see natural things here on Earth change in minute ways that govern their very existence, so an entire universe can improve its own odds of survival. No, the universe does not consciously adapt any more than one of your animals or plants consciously adapted to its environment. "The survival of the fittest" applies to natural things as well as living things. It has applied to the Big Bang, too.

In the infinite reach of time, billions of universes have been created that did _not_, in fact, achieve the exact critical rate of expansion, and so were shorter lived than *your* universe. Nevertheless, the day will come when your universe stops expanding and begins the incredibly long process of collapsing. In 100 trillion years or so, your universe will end in a Big Bang and instantly be reborn in a new universe that probably will not expand at the same rate as yours, and as a result, it will be either longer or shorter lived.

58. WHY DID GOD CREATE HUMANS, WHO ONLY WRECK ALL THE OTHER BEAUTIFUL THINGS ON EARTH?

God was going through a phase then. It was an experiment. God regrets it and has moved on. It will all be over in a few billion years.

Okay, that's a _joke_. Don't look so glum! God does not go through "phases" like some hormonal teenager, and that's a good thing for you!

There are no <u>humans</u> on other planets, although there are so-called "intelligent beings." A lot of the "mistakes" on Earth have been corrected elsewhere. Not all of them, though. For instance, golf is everywhere, and you wouldn't _believe_ some of the bunkers. (God's favorite fairway is the 471st in the galaxy Gknisfudn.)

But music is everywhere, too! Music is universal, and so are the laws of math and physics. Every galaxy has atomic energy, and gravity, and electricity, and television. With commercials. But not everybody gets cable.

So, what was the question again? Oh right, another everything-is-God's-fault question. God did not create humans, but merely created the environment in which humans became possible. Do you really wreck ALL the beauty of the Earth? You are part of that beauty, you know. Some of you sure do wreck more than your fair share, but don't blame God for that.

59. GOD, WHY DID YOU CHOOSE TO CREATE EACH PERSON DIFFERENTLY? MORE SPECIFICALLY, WHAT IS THE PURPOSE OF CREATING SUCH COMPLEX PERSONALITIES IN EACH INDIVIDUAL? WAS IT PERHAPS TO TEACH US HOW TO LOVE ONE ANOTHER? *

In the universe, there are millions of species that *don't* have complex personalities, and very few species that do. God is not a cosmic Frank Lloyd Wright building God's Dream Planet, with file drawers stuffed with blueprints, one for each species. God is merely the chef, creating the primordial soup and waiting to see what emerges. Love was not one of its ingredients. Love among people simply happened as human beings married intellect with the natural affinity of one member of a species for other members of the same species. We hate to go all clinical on you, but God is more than a little sick of the fat little arrow-shooting cherub image.

Which is not to say that love is a bad thing. Mutual attraction is a big deal all the way up and down the chain of creation. Beings on other planets experience love, too, and God is all for it. What we do not want is for people to think of God as any of the following:

- The ultimate reality-show host, manipulating Earthlings like they were contestants on "Survivor" or "The Dating Game"
- Barry White
- Dr. Ruth Westheimer
- A yenta (matchmaker), or
- Eligible to date

60. WAS IT HARD TO MAKE SIX BILLION PEOPLE AND EACH ONE DIFFERENT THAN THE OTHER? BECAUSE SOMETIMES THERE ARE TWINS.

Diversity is the one of the best things about creation, but individual differences are not planned or designed. Given the almost infinite number of possible combinations of features, skin colors, organ sizes, hairstyles and colors, etc., it's actually pretty amazing that so many people resemble each other. Even God can't tell the difference between some celebrities and their less famous look-alikes.

61. WHY ONLY MALE AND FEMALE HUMAN BEINGS? WE COULD HAVE USED AT LEAST TWO OTHERS!

We are perplexed as to how you might be able to "use" other genders. That's a little scary. But the answer is that there are only two genders. Isn't it hard enough raising sons and daughters? Imagine if you had four children, one of each gender. "Stop hitting your sister and… thing and… other thing!"

62. IF GOD DID NOT EXIST, WOULD THE WORLD GO ON?

No. We ARE the world. We are the children. No, wait a minute, that's a song. Okay, the real answer is, God is irrelevant. The universe and everything that happens in it goes on by itself. If it was necessary for God to start the cosmos, then wasn't it also necessary for something to start God? If there was a void, then God must have been part of the void, which means God was nothing. If you accept that God is *not* nothing, then the universe must have existed before God, and it would also exist without God. I think I'm getting a headache.

63. ARE HUMANS THE HIGHEST LIFE FORM ON EARTH?

It's not a contest. Why does one have to be the highest? To God, all life is the same. In fact, all creation is the same. It's just as hard to create a *rock* out of nothing as it is to create a person.

Humans, in fact, are not even the DOMINANT life form on Earth. Cats and dogs are dominant, because without even having to learn to think or invent, they have gotten you humans to give them everything. You do all the work, and all they have to do is enjoy life. Remember, these animals survive just fine without you, but they've put you to work to make their lives really cushy. Of course, for them, the downside is being neutered, but they're willing to make that trade.

64. If I may follow up that answer, WHY DID GOD PICK HUMANS TO HAVE A CONSCIOUSNESS?

Actually, God first thought it should be a different species. But then that opposable thumb idea came up during evolution, and God just decided to go with it, and the next thing you know... BAM! Human consciousness.

65. ARE WE ALONE IN THE UNIVERSE?

It's curious — and commendable — that you would ask this question that way. Others want to know if there is other life, particularly intelligent life, in the universe. Yet you, instead of wanting to know if there is something else "out there," have phrased it differently, seeing pretty much the entire planet Earth as a single entity. By saying "we," you have shown that you see the connection between yourself and the rest of the inhabitants of your planet. Read on.

66. IS THERE LIFE ON OTHER PLANETS? IF SO, WHAT KIND OF LIFE? AND I HAVE A FOLLOW-UP QUESTION WHEN YOU'RE DONE.

You humans are so arrogant to think that you might be IT for the whole universe! Get over yourselves!

There is definitely life on other planets. And on many of them, I, your humble press secretary, would be considered a hunk. If you mean, is there *intelligent* life on other planets, the answer is yes. But we wonder, given whom you Earthlings select as your leaders sometimes, if there is intelligent life on *this* planet?

"Life" is a tricky concept. What does it mean for something to be alive? Even on Earth, most living things have no consciousness, no sense of self. On other planets, some things that God would consider "living" might not be recognized as life by Earthlings.

What is your follow-up question?

67. WILL EARTHLINGS EVER MAKE DIRECT CONTACT WITH INTELLIGENT BEINGS FROM ANOTHER PLANET? WHAT ARE THEY LIKE?

It is, as we've pointed out elsewhere in this book, arrogance that is the defining characteristic of Earth people. It is, to God, your least attractive quality. Somehow, in a cosmos that is infinite and in which all possibilities are unlimited, Earthlings have decided that God favored them as the ultimate creation. If that were not what at least some Earthlings believe, then why would they believe that God made humans in God's own image? (Let's not even discuss that some people think that the human male – "man" – in particular is the spit and image of God. If God *did* choose to take on an appearance, it would not have stubble.)

Try to lose, for the moment, the arrogant notion that humans are some incredibly special species in the whole of the cosmos (recognizing, of course, that something without end can never actually be "whole"). Granted, humans are the most *intelligent* and environment-controlling species on Earth. That's not saying much. Look at your competition! Bivalves. Crustaceans. Insects. Guppies. Dogs. Dogwood trees. Redwood trees. Orchids. Most of these things have no greater intelligence than a rock. (Not to insult rocks, of which God would be extremely proud, if God felt pride.) So, big whoop – you humans can kick the butt of a frog, or even an ape, in an intelligence contest, and you can so totally control the environment of all other things on your planet, that you've managed to exterminate entire species.

But I digress. Look again at the universe. Of COURSE there are other intelligent beings out there. And in terms of intelligence and understanding of the cosmos, you humans are way down the list.

When you say you desire contact with intelligent life from other planets, you expect that contact to come in one of the forms with which you are familiar: sound or visual image, in a written or spoken language, or through mathematical constants (including music). But why limit the possibilities? You see, you are so new on the evolutionary scale, you do not yet know the other ways that beings can communicate. Those who believe that Earth has been "visited" by intelligent life from elsewhere are absolutely correct. However, they haven't really got a clue as to the nature of those visits. They're thinking crop circles and flying saucers. That is so "inside the box." The so-called "aliens" from other planets are here all the time, and they – at least some of them – communicate with you all the time, but their means of communication are beyond your comprehension. (See Questions 122 and 123 about ghosts.)

For that same reason, it is impossible to describe in terms you'd understand the nature of alien beings. Some, of course, are exactly what you see in "Star Wars" and "Close Encounters of the Third Kind." Any way you imagine a living thing could look, there is such a thing somewhere in the cosmos. There is also intelligent life that requires no physical body. It is informed energy that meets all the standard definitions of "life," and makes decisions that affect its environment.

There are two kinds of "things" in the cosmos: matter and energy. You accept, because you are the proof of it, that some matter can become "intelligent," defined as having the ability to recognize and control, to some extent, its existence. If matter can have intelligence, why can't energy? Most matter is without intelligence, and so is most energy. But *some* matter gains intellectual capability, and, I'm pleased to report, so does some energy.

Is this starting to get too technical? Let's just say that there is an infinite variety of "life" in the cosmos, and that the diversity here on Earth is nothing compared to the diversity throughout your universe and the rest of the cosmos.

Now, it is interesting to note that *some* humans communicate, unknowingly, with the alien visitors. These people are most receptive when they are asleep, which is why there is no interactive communication, no real dialogue that takes place. Except for the aliens here on your Earth, you will almost certainly never communicate with other intelligent beings. The distances between you are simply too great, and you are nowhere near having the means to travel to their planets.

68. DOES GOD HAVE ANY REGRET FOR CREATING US HUMANS, CONSIDERING THE MESS WE HAVE MADE OF THIS PLANET AND THE AMOUNT OF FIGHTING WE DO AMONGST OURSELVES? HOW COULD GOD HAVE MADE US BETTER? WE CAN'T BE THE ONLY BEINGS IN THE UNIVERSE WITH OUR ABILITY FOR THOUGHT. THERE MUST BE OTHERS WHO HAVE MANAGED BETTER THAN WE HAVE, WHO AREN'T SO PETTY AND SELF-CENTERED.

Made you better for *what?* It is just your perception that God is not satisfied with Earth people exactly as you are. What evidence do you have that God has abandoned you?

You are, with all the things YOU call imperfections, doing reasonably well. Not all intelligent life everywhere in the cosmos is doing as well as you humans. The thing you need to wonder about is, what does *God* mean by intelligent life? For that matter, what does "doing well" mean in God's terms? In other words, to what are you being compared?

God is not a person, does not react to comparative values the way a person would. So, God does not get "pleased" with things, per se. Forget what the Bible says, that God created a few things, then stepped back to look at it like some Renaissance artist, and decided to be pleased. Remember, the word "please" means to give or derive *pleasure.* God is not a pleasure-seeker, out looking for the Big Thrill. God creates what God creates, with no ability to forecast how it's going to turn out and almost no ability to *affect* the way it turns out. What happens, happens. *Que sera sera,* as the song goes.

Okay, so that's the *lecture* part of the answer. God is big on caveats. But God also wants you to know that you *can* compare yourselves to other intelligent-life societies and

65

find that you come up short. For example, some "alien" societies have learned to sustain life and control their environment without polluting it, without needlessly destroying other species of life on their planet, and without causing the resources that sustain their lives to dwindle and disappear. Because they have no fear of vital resources becoming scarce, they have no wars, no jealousy of one another. God is sure that to you, this place sounds like paradise. Keep in mind, though, that the resources vital to _their_ existence are not necessarily the same things you humans require. The resources you need most – water, food, shelter – are not 100 percent renewable. Your supplies diminish bit by bit, faster and faster as your population grows. The good news is that these "paradise-dwelling" aliens were, at some point in their evolution, exactly like you Earthlings. So, there is hope for you yet to achieve a paradise here on Earth, but it will take a very long time.

You must realize, though, that you also could be a lot worse off. Some _other_ alien societies have started with all the same factors as Earth, and wiped themselves out very quickly, virtually destroying their planet's hopes for diverse life forever into the future, when their planet will be consumed in a cosmic fireball, as all planets eventually are, to be reborn as a new planet in an entirely new solar system. (Uh, wait a minute here while I wipe that cataclysmic gleam from my eye.) You see, the cosmos recreates itself again and again and again without end.

Now, as for regrets... well, that's another human emotion that is not part of God. God understands what human emotions _are_, but God does not experience such feelings. And it's a good thing for you that God does not. If God could feel regret, then God could also feel pride. Right? If something is happening that you regret, and then the situation changes, you may feel pride if you had something to do with it. "Hey, look. That thing I created. It's _working_ now!" Or maybe you'd feel relief. But that implies that you can feel happy or sad, and that you fluctuate between the two. Let me make this _really_ clear. You DON'T want a God that fluctuates. Imagine the most manic-depressive person you know, and now... give them all the power in the universe.

Fortunately, God does not feel emotion. As we said before, God does not control what happens on a planet (or even _inside_ a planet). God is time. Time passes and things change constantly. No day on Earth is the same as the day before. There are new beings – plants and people and other animals – that were not there at all the day before, and other beings that have died and will return to the cosmos for rebirth as something else (most likely without intelligence). Things have moved from place to place, resources have been consumed. And the perceived quality of life on a planet changes daily, too, as beings interact with one another.

So, no, God has no regrets. God knows things could be different on Earth and that some changes would please most Earthlings, while displeasing some other species on Earth. No change occurs in a vacuum. There is, as UU's say, an interdependent web of all existence. It could be better. It could be worse. If you don't like it, you must do what you can to change it.

69. That was a very long answer, but it begs a follow-up question. I'M CURIOUS WHAT AN IMPROVED HUMAN MODEL MIGHT BE LIKE.

The "improved human model" – Humans 2.0, if you will – is not something God ordains, but something that you can bring about yourselves.

What might an improved human model look like? God has no blueprint for an ideal being. No animals or plants anywhere in the cosmos are immortal. Everything dies eventually. The seemingly most content beings are in societies in which all members are selfless. There is no greed, no jealousy, yet there is still ambition – the desire to work hard for the common good. Imagine a society of ants that also has vast intelligence *and* opposable thumbs! There are such societies in the cosmos, and they know better than to try to contact Earth. (See the next question about how humans will evolve.)

70. HOW WILL HUMANS EVOLVE IN THE FUTURE?

God cannot predict with any certainty, because there are so many factors that impact evolution. However, if you continue on the current path, you will likely find that you continue to lose your brutish characteristics in favor of your most cerebral. In other words, you will continue to be less like cavemen, with their great physical strength needed to survive, and you will rely more on your ability to think.

Your best indicator of evolution is: allergies. The most highly evolved of you have the most allergies. These are your body's reaction to things it cannot tolerate, things it wants to do without. As your body becomes accustomed to doing without certain things, you pass on those characteristics to your descendants, and they don't need those things, either. Over a million years or so, the list of things you can do without will grow, until your body grows less vital and the powers of your mind reign supreme. Either that, OR... you'll grow feathers and learn to fly.

Another potential target for evolution is nationalism. Pride in one's homeland is so ingrained in humanity that one must conclude it is a natural condition for Earthlings, something that evolved naturally and unavoidably. In the days before widespread travel and mass media, it made sense for people to believe that where they lived, no matter what troubles they may have encountered, was the best place for them to be. The advent of airplanes and cars, of radio and film and television, made it conceivable that nationalism would wane. Pride of homeland is sincere and deep in most people. Channel that pride to sports, as in the Olympics, and it's a good thing. Channel it to property rights and corporate profits, and you will wipe each other out. Evolution, far from stamping it out, seems to have made nationalism grow stronger.

71. WHEN GOD CREATED LIFE FORMS, WHY WERE DIGESTIVE SYSTEMS DESIGNED TO MAKE WASTE PRODUCTS? WOULDN'T TOTAL ABSORPTION HAVE BEEN MORE EFFICIENT?

You should probably be glad that God is not an efficiency expert, or human life would be very different. Life, you see, is a byproduct of the cosmos, not its focus. Life forms exist in infinite variety, and some actually DO absorb and recycle their own waste. But that was not by God's design. See Question 48 about quantum mechanics.

72. WHERE DO THE GREAT INVENTIONS OF HISTORY COME FROM? DOES GOD PLANT THE IDEAS IN THE MINDS OF THE GREAT THINKERS AND INVENTORS?

God does not control any aspect of what humans do. Take all the inventions and discoveries of human history. You guys did that all on your own, but some people don't get that. They think that God knows all there is to know and has always known it from the beginning of time, but then God decided to p•a•r•c•e•l it out to humans a little bit at a time. What kind of sicko would do that? No, God pretty much threw the universe together and has spent the last 100 billion years organizing it. Kind of like a family that moves into a new house and takes a really long time to unpack and put things away. God still has lots of boxes to open.

73. I DID NOT CHOOSE TO BE BORN, BUT I WAS BORN, NAKED AND IGNORANT. I DID NOT PLAN OR CONCEIVE MYSELF. ALL THAT I AM, I WAS GIVEN; ALL THAT I KNOW, I LEARNED. I ASK MYSELF QUESTIONS ABOUT THE MEANING OF LIFE, AND ANSWERS SEEM TO APPEAR, ANSWERS I WAS NOT BORN KNOWING. CAN THESE ANSWERS COME FROM ANYONE BUT GOD, AND IF NOT FROM GOD, THEN DOES THAT MAKE ME GREATER THAN THAT WHICH CREATED ME?

"Greater?" Such comparative terms have no meaning to God. You, as a physical being with emotions and organs and birth and death, can do things God will never do. Does that make you greater? God is eternal and everywhere. Does that make you lesser? If your answers to the meaning of life were correct – which they are not – would that make you greater than God? If your answers are wrong, does it make you any less significant? Life is not a television game show in which the right answers win you points. You are not competing against or for God. You are what you are, no more and no less. God does not give you the answers, only the ability to ask the questions.

74. WHAT INSPIRED GOD TO CREATE MUSIC AND HUMOR?

God DIDN'T create those directly. For one thing, God does not *get* inspired. God is not like a person sitting around worrying about Creator's Block when suddenly... WHAM... inspiration strikes.

Because it is based on mathematical constants, music is everywhere in the cosmos. Music is the sound of the cosmos talking. Humor is also a natural byproduct of the universe. You'll notice that most species on Earth have no sense of humor, because to appreciate absurdity, which is the source of all humor, you have to recognize what is logical and what is absurd. Humor is more finely developed on some other planets, where the current most popular joke is, "How many Earthlings does it take to change a light bulb?" and the answer is, "Only one very rich one who can afford to have the old light bulb recalled."

75. I KNOW, I KNOW, I'VE BEEN A BIT CRITICAL OF LATE WHEN I THINK OF YOU. TRULY, YOUR GODSHIP, HAVE YOU LOST INTEREST IN THE FABULOUS VARIETY OF YOUR CREATIONS HERE? IT SEEMS YOU STARTED US UP AND THEN HOPED WE WOULD EVOLVE ON OUR OWN. *

Bingo! God hasn't "lost" interest at all. God never had any to begin with. The idea of being "interested" in something is a human trait. So is "hope." God did not create things and then, like some child making a birthday wish, "hope" it would turn out all right. Life is what it is. You get the chance to make the most out of it. The rest of God's creations are doing just fine on their own. You've been fine for thousands of years without God actually being there for you. If you prefer to continue thinking that God intervenes in human life, go ahead. Be our guest. It doesn't hurt for kids to believe in Santa Claus, either.

76. WERE PEOPLE CREATED TO SERVE AND TO PLEASE GOD?

Is that what you think of God? Do you believe that God craves pleasure, and that in the vast, infinite cosmos, Earth people – and perhaps other beings – were created as a kind of "Upstairs, Downstairs," Valhalla Version? Even to ask the question is arrogance.

Just looking at your universe alone, there are uncountable species of plants and animals, some with greater intelligence than Earthlings. In this context, you humans are incredibly puny. Not insignificant, just small, even at several billion of you.

Look at your history. Over the thousands of years people have been around, you have not exactly covered yourselves in glory. It's been one war after another, and when you're not fighting each other with weapons, you're busy hating each other, feeding your bigotry, and committing horribly immoral acts. What part of this wonderful past do you think would "please" God?

Not that it would matter if you were the most selfless, well-behaved species in the cosmos. God is not a pleasure-seeker, and does not judge any creations. God does not need your approval, and you do not need God's.

God does not even care if people pay no attention to God. In fact, God prefers it that way. Less hypocrisy. Some of the most despicable acts in history have been committed by people who worship God the most fervently. How could God possibly be pleased by someone who claims to love God but is busy destroying God's creations? God does not need servants, but does respect those who respect not God, but everything else without exception.

IV. LIFE
Or, WAITER, THERE'S A HAIR IN MY PRIMORDIAL SOUP

One question comes up again and again, often in different forms. As one person asked, ""How is it that your minions credit you with all the good things that happen but never fault you for the bad? For example, you cause a terrible tornado that wipes out part of a city, killing a dozen people. Someone who was spared from the disaster runs over to a reporter and 'thanks you' for having spared them. Never is it mentioned that you must also be responsible for having created the tornado in the first place."

In a different take on the same question, a teenage girl asked, "I'd like to know why, all of a sudden, things are going wonderfully for me, but my best friend's cat is dying, she was sexually abused by her boyfriend whom she dumped, and now she feels guilty about it, she's having trouble in school, and her life is falling around her. But she's a wonderful person and deserves everything in the world. I want to know why she gets complete chaos and I'm suddenly so lucky?"

No matter how it is phrased, it boils down to the same question:

77. WHY DO BAD THINGS HAPPEN TO GOOD PEOPLE, AND VICE VERSA?

Because bad things... and good things... just happen. God didn't plan it that way. There's a lot more randomness in the universe than you can ever imagine. If God controlled every event, every thought, every breath of every person, would that make life _better_... or worse? We have to make a choice:

- Control everything
- Control some things
- Control nothing

God follows the middle ground, minds the big stuff, and lets the rest work itself out. We don't like to see innocent people die, or accidents happen, but the alternative is worse, believe me. You know how some people think the government controls too much stuff? Well, think of what it would be like if _God_ controlled everything!

Some people talk of God's Plan for the World. There is no "Plan." Everyone wants to think of God as some kind of architect or engineer who lays everything out nice and neat before proceeding. That's so Late-Middle-Ages. God is more like a kid in a candy store, trying out a little of everything in more or less random order. Something good happens somewhere, like a really great harvest, and people are all worshipful and thanking God (sometimes in very self-demeaning ways), when really God had nothing to do with it. It just happened.

Or maybe it's not so much that something _good_ happens as that you avoid something _bad_ happening. Recently — and this is a true story which I observed on American television — a suicide bomber in Israel blew himself up and killed a whole lot of Israelis, and one woman who had been at that same exact spot just seconds earlier was loudly thanking God for sparing her! Say what? She thinks God just killed all these people right next to her, or allowed them to be killed, and all she can think about is *herself* and that somehow, as God was busy killing all those people, *she* was selected to live? What arrogance! God didn't decide who got killed and who lived! How sick would that be?

So, here's the thing. God is NOT VAIN. If you were God, all powerful, everywhere in the cosmos at the same time, would it matter to you if people worshipped you or not? No way! It's actually kind of insulting that some people think God will punish those who don't worship God. What they are really suggesting is that God is petty, that being the Supreme Being of the universe is not enough, and that God needs you all to be God's toady. When bad things happen, it's not because God is angry, or vindictive, or feeling disrespected, OR that God is "calling that person home." God never ends anyone's life just so they can be with God. So, worship God or curse God, it's all the same to God. God has bigger fish to fry, or as we like to say, "Bigger stars to burn."

78. WHAT DOES GOD CONSIDER GOD'S GREATEST GIFT TO THE LIVING?

The ability to sleep. Actually, the *necessity* to sleep. Imagine how different life would be if nobody slept, if no living things slept (or the equivalent). In some ways, things might be better. If Einstein had thousands of extra hours of wakefulness (and could be alert through them all), imagine what other contributions he might have made. The same can be said of hundreds of other great thinkers and doers.

But there would also be a huge downside to constant wakefulness. People would "burn out" much sooner. God experimented on another planet with intelligent beings who did not sleep or rest. They did not live nearly as long as Earthlings, and their civilization lasted but a few thousand years.

Sleep not only helps you grow when you're young, and gain energy throughout your life, but it also lets you cope with pain and fear and all other negative emotions. It lets your brain access images and thoughts you might otherwise miss, including virtual visits with people who are far away or deceased. Not a bad gift, eh?

79. WHAT DOES IT ALL MEAN? WHAT IS THE MEANING OF LIFE?

Every time I eavesdrop to find out what Earthlings want to know, that <u>always</u> comes up. If I told you the meaning, then what? You'd probably get all depressed, or you'd want to argue about it.

God finds it curious that anything that comes into existence would question its own existence. Why does life have to have a purpose? In any event, if there *is* a purpose, no living person has ever discovered what it is. So, if it's impossible to discern, why waste time in the pursuit? Isn't that basically *defeating* the purpose? Why not just accept life as a wonderful mystery? Do you really need to know your place in the cosmos, or to know how the universe began? Instead, be astonished at the universe and its complexities. Marvel at it the way a child marvels at a magic show. And, in the end, that's exactly what life is – the most wonderful magic show. Sure, part of you wants to know how a magician does those fantastic illusions. But you also know that if you learn the "trick," the wonder will go out of it. The fun will fade. It's an illusion; that's all you need or want to know. Some things are better left unexplained. Life is one of those things.

If you were *forced* to guess at the purpose of life, you'd have to say that it was to die, because that's the <u>only</u> thing that every living thing has in common. If that's NOT the answer, then there must be lots of purposes, since there is nothing else that living beings share in common. The number of purposes must be almost infinite, then, right? There are so many different beings. Each Earthling could have a different purpose. So, who's going to determine that purpose? God? Unh-unh. YOU determine it, through your actions. Dying is not a purpose. It's a result.

However, if you want to know what God expects of you, it is this:

- Embrace your humanity. Never forget that you are basically just an animal, but that you, alone among Earth's animals and other living things, have the resources to control your environment and to interact with others of your species with intelligence and for your mutual benefit. Do not squander these resources.
- Do nothing to harm other people.
- Live the Golden Rule.
- Be better than you have to be.
- Keep a sense of humor with you at all times.
- Don't be too hard on yourself.
- Cherish the past, but don't live there.
- Try to leave the world a better place than you found it, even if only just a little.
- Don't be too quick to judge others.
- And never end a sentence with a preposition.

80. WHAT IS YOUR SOUL?

Your great philosopher, René Descartes, said, "I think; therefore I am." The part of you about which that statement is true is your soul.

81. May I ask a follow-up question, Jeremiah? DO ANIMALS HAVE SOULS?

Some do. Most don't. You're not going to hold that against them, are you?

82. WHY IS LIFE SUCH A STRUGGLE?

One problem with human life is that trust has to be earned constantly. You can never relax. No matter how good you are or how good you've been, you are always, to someone, a stranger. You can say, "I am a good, kind person, and I have the credentials to prove it," and they will immediately determine that you are a homicidal, child-molesting maniac.

In life, no one trusts you implicitly, except maybe your mother, if you're lucky. You have to prove yourself constantly, because you will meet new people throughout your life, right to the very last day. That's the reason that the idea of God and an afterlife appeals to some people. They look forward to the day when they can relax, and they figure they ought to be able to relax once they've made it to heaven, because then all the other angels can just look at them and know they are good.

Life is such a struggle because you are trapped inside your own mind and body. You can bond with friends and family, but you can never be someone else. In the worst of times, sleep is the only relief, and sometimes even that can be disturbed by your thoughts in the form of dreams. Your intellect is your enemy. Most animals and all plants have no sense of the struggle of life. The very thoughts that let you control your environment make you aware of how little control you have. And so you convince yourself that you are beset by trouble and struggling to survive, painfully aware that no matter what you do, you must lose the battle of survival. That thought is too rude to contemplate, so you hope that the end is not the end, that there is something more.

Instead, relax. Make every day of your life the best day of your life. Don't despair. Today's troubles are tomorrow's history lesson. As long as you are alive and in good health, don't despair.

83. MANY PEOPLE SAY EVERYTHING HAPPENS FOR A REASON. IS THAT TRUE?

Some things that people (and other animals) do, they do as part of a plan or a process, but that's not what you mean, is it? You mean when something unexpected happens, it was part of a plan unknown at the time it occurred. That is total nuclear waste.

In order for things to happen for a reason, it would mean that future events were somehow planned. But by whom? God does not script your life and then direct you like some supernatural Alfred Hitchcock. There is no "storyboard" of your life (and the lives of everyone you meet) tucked away in a Jupiter-sized lateral file. Things do not happen for a reason, but the effect of each action is that other things happen that would not otherwise have occurred. Thus, everything you do causes what comes after, but not as part of any great plan.

This fact should not upset anyone, particularly those people who are inclined to see the good and bad things in their life as part of God's plan for them. They should take comfort in the fact that when bad things happen to them, there was no intention to it; God did not throw obstacles in their path. And when good things happen to them, it's because they really deserve it or were at least ready for something good; God did not suddenly decide to reward them.

84. IN "THE PURPOSE-DRIVEN LIFE" BY RICK WARREN, THE OPENING PARAGRAPH SAYS, "THIS BOOK IS DEDICATED TO YOU. BEFORE YOU WERE BORN, GOD PLANNED *THIS MOMENT* IN YOUR LIFE. IT IS NO ACCIDENT THAT YOU ARE HOLDING THIS BOOK. GOD *LONGS* FOR YOU TO DISCOVER THE LIFE HE CREATED YOU TO LIVE HERE ON EARTH, AND FOREVER IN ETERNITY." MY QUESTION IS, IS THIS TRUE?

Yes, it IS true... That's exactly what the opening paragraph says. The rest of it, of course, is what we call "meteor chunks." You should be delighted to know that God does not plan *anything* that happens. (See Question 75 about God's interest in humans.)

85. SOME PEOPLE SAY THERE ARE NO "ACCIDENTS," THAT PEOPLE SECRETLY WANT THE ACCIDENT TO HAPPEN. ARE THERE REALLY ACCIDENTS?

Pretty much everything that happens does so by accident. You don't think God has nothing to do but plan little mishaps, do you? A lot of people blame "the devil" for the nasty little surprises of daily life, or even the nasty BIG surprises. Well, as some of you Earth people say, "That dog don't hunt," or as we like to say, "That black hole don't suck." (See Question 37 about Satan.)

Now, of course, you might be referring to the problems some people have of doing the wrong thing pretty much regularly. God refuses to speculate on what goes on in someone's mind when they do things. Oh, did we forget to mention that God does not read minds? God has no clue what you're thinking, so don't worry about it. A lot of folks worry about having freedom of speech, and that's certainly an important right, recognized in all advanced societies throughout the cosmos. But freedom of _thought_ is another such right.

Many people argue passionately for their freedom to say whatever they think, as long as others aren't physically hurt by it. And yet many of those same people are perfectly willing to surrender their freedom to _think_ whatever they want without batting an eyelash. They believe God knows when they have an evil thought, or a jealous thought, or a lustful thought, and it drives them nuts, judging from what they say out loud. (By the way, there's no point in praying silently. God can't "hear" it.) They're worrying for nothing. Those magicians on TV can't really read your mind, and neither can God, although God CAN do a pretty fair spoon-bending trick. The only thing that really matters is what you SAY and DO, not what you think before you say it or do it. So, don't spend any time feeling guilty for

84

what your mind dreams up. Heck, that's one of the perks of *having* a mind – that it can take you all over the place.

So, back to the question at hand, which is whether people secretly want accidents to happen, and the answer is that God just does not know what people secretly want. However, in the natural world, beyond the control of intelligent beings, accidents happen all the time. A meteor crashing into a planet is not part of some grand plan. God does not control the planets and other objects the way a little kid controls a model train set, deliberately putting things on a collision course just to watch it go BOOM! It's part of the grand chaos that exists everywhere.

86. I'd like to follow up on that answer. WE CALL MANY THINGS THAT HAPPEN TOGETHER A "COINCIDENCE." DO THESE THINGS HAPPEN BY MISTAKE OR BY YOUR DESIGN?

Basically, this question gets the same answer as the last one. There's not much difference, when you come right down to it, between an "accident" and a "coincidence," except that a coincidence may be two things happening at the same time, but not happening to each other or in the same place. God does not coordinate two unrelated events to occur simultaneously. God's philosophy is, "If-it-isn't-happening-right-now-I-don't-want-to-know-about-it." God is essentially Everything That Is Happening In This Moment Everywhere In The Cosmos. There is no "yesterday" to God, and there is no "tomorrow." So planning pretty much is NOT going to happen. Time just happens. Change just happens. Coincidences... oh, you get the idea.

87. ARE ALL THE MYRIAD OCCURRENCES ON OUR
PLANET PART OF A LEARNING PROCESS
ESPECIALLY GEARED TO HUMANS, AND IF SO, TO
WHAT END?

You humans are so fixated on the parenting model.
Whether or not your own parents were there for you, you
have this notion that parents are supposed to care for you,
nurture you, and teach you how to prepare for life. That's a
very good model for people, but a very poor one for God.
People cannot imagine a creator who is not like a human
parent, a God that could create something but not care
about it.

God is nothing like the loving, nurturing parent that
Earth people have fantasized for thousands of generations.
God has no plan for you and is not preparing you for
something else. If you learn how you want to live from
observing the world around you, great, but don't assume
that what you learn is part of a master plan.

88. WHY DOES GOD TREAT OLD PEOPLE SO BADLY?

Should things last forever? Most things start out weak or unstable, then get stronger, and then fade. Stars gather intensity, then burn themselves out; saplings add layers of bark for strength, and then collapse under their own weight. Nothing is permanent; even your universe will eventually implode only to be recreated in another Big Bang. Old people have it no worse than old stars or trees. There is pain in aging, but there would be more pain in not aging. (See Question 8, Does God Age?)

Your concern for the quality of life as people age also relates to Question 79 about the meaning of life. So many Earth people hang on to life as if their only goal is to live as long as possible, no matter how miserable their existence. Why? Are they expecting some sort of prize? You show mercy to animals that suffer, but you flinch at giving other people the same respect as their pets. You won't even let or help a dying person end his or her own life. (See Question 173 about suicide.) You think it is better to drug them into a stupor to relieve their pain and then exhibit them like some animated curiosity. So you think God treats old people badly? You're not so nice yourself.

89. WHERE ARE MY UNMATCHED SOCKS?

They have been donated to a galaxy of beings with cold feet.

90. DO PEOPLE HAVE A DESTINY OR PREDETERMINED FATE?

Nope. Although God *knew* you were going to ask that question. Think about _that_.

91. DOES HISTORY REPEAT ITSELF?

Oh, yes. At this very moment, in another galaxy, General Custer and his men are being massacred. The only difference is that this time they are dying with their boots *off.*

No, the real answer is that history does not repeat itself. It just seems that way. (See Question 86 about coincidences.) Time is infinite, forwards and backwards. It is not looped in a circle. Time past never comes back around again anywhere, although thanks to the properties of light, it is possible to see today something that happened millions of years ago, such as the explosion of a star. So, events that happen occur just once. There may be very similar events, but never the same event. Although, Albert Einstein said insanity is "doing the same thing over and over again and expecting different results." If you do the same things under the same circumstances, you can expect history to repeat itself.

92. DO YOU GIVE US JUST ONE LIFETIME TO DO IT RIGHT, OR DO YOU GIVE US AS MANY AS IT TAKES TO DO IT RIGHT? *

One crack at it is all you get. Life is not some game on the midway at the amusement park where you can keep trying until you win. Therefore, it is extremely important that you do your best with what you've got now. Yes, it means that cruel people are, in the end, no worse off than kind, honest people. But which person has enjoyed life more? To get the most from your life *during* your life, you must participate, and you must be good and peaceful and loving. You do not need to be rich or good-looking or well educated or born in the "right" country to live a full and rewarding life. You must, however, not rely on getting a second chance. There is no afterlife and no reincarnation. If you are not happy now, you have the power to change that. Don't put off trying.

93. WHEN WILL THERE BE WORLD PEACE?

Is there peace in _your_ life? If so, then that's as good as it's going to get. God is not in the prediction business and will not speculate on when or if people will learn to live in peace. First, you have to _want_ to live in peace. Second, you must allow others to have things you don't. God is not very optimistic that people will ever be like that.

Another obstacle to peace is that it is not as compelling and entertaining and interesting as war. Look how you Earthlings are attracted to war and to warriors. War makes a better "story" than peace, even though peace is the better way to live. War is more seductive. It's sexier. Peace is not sexy.

94. But Jeremiah, what about... Oh, may I ask a follow-up question? I UNDERSTAND GOD CAN'T MAKE PREDICTIONS, BUT CAN GOD TELL US WHETHER THERE *MIGHT BE* PEACE IN THE MIDDLE EAST? IS IT POSSIBLE?

The one thing you know for sure once you've seen the cosmos is, *every*thing is possible. There have been too many twists and turns already in Earthbound societies and on other planets with intelligent life for God to say what will and will not happen.

The thing about the Middle East is that everybody involved is doing something wrong. It doesn't matter who started it, who was the first to do something bad to the other. Nobody is willing to just stop and say, "Enough already." It will probably take many more generations before ALL sides are willing to forget the past. Or it may never happen.

We in God's administration are pretty amazed that no one has figured out yet that the whole Middle East thing is like God's greatest practical joke, that is, if God were practical and could make jokes! I mean, c'mon. Three of the world's biggest, baddest religions all have their most holy shrines within the same tiny plot of land, and you all think that someone wasn't just fooling around? See, this is <u>*exactly*</u> what I had in mind when I say that you don't really want a God that thinks and feels and intervenes. (See Questions 38 and 75.)

95. DO YOU WEEP WHEN PEOPLE KILL NON-HUMAN CREATURES FOR SPORT?

Weep? No. But neither does God cheer. God has no emotions, which is as it should be, for everything that comes into existence will also pass out of it. Every living thing dies, every star eventually explodes, every creation ends. If God could feel each passing the way you humans do, the cosmos would be a place of infinite sadness, and God would cease creating.

The curious point of this question, though, is what constitutes killing for sport? Do you expect God to be an all-knowing Judge Judy, able to discern exactly what is in the mind of the killer, what reason they have for killing? Should God smile on the hunter who eats the prey and throw lightning bolts at the hunter who leaves the meat for other creatures? No, God does not weep or judge you in any way, BUT... that does not make it right for you to destroy any of God's creations on a whim. If you do, when you do, you must answer to your fellow humans, but not to God.

96. IS HUMANKIND DOOMED TO DESTROY ITSELF? WILL WE DESTROY EARTH?

Not necessarily, but God is not the one pulling the strings here. When you say "doomed," you imply that the fate of the world is predetermined, that someone or something is in charge and already knows the outcome. That's the same false assumption that leads people to act superstitiously. For example, we know some people who won't watch their favorite team on TV because they think that their watching will cause the team to lose! Did you ever avoid doing something because you felt that just by being around, you could cause bad things to happen? We hate to keep using the word "arrogant," but it certainly applies here. The universe is not reordered just because you exist.

But let's face it – you Earth people are not exactly taking perfect care of the Earth's resources or treating each other with the greatest respect. Keep treating each other and the Earth badly, and, yeah, you're probably doomed. It's not too late to avoid that, though. Unfortunately, you figured out nuclear power before you evolved to a higher level of intelligence. So now, all kinds of relatively primitive humans have the power to blow things up, and there's no shortage of people crazy enough to want to try. That includes a bunch of people who think their ticket to heaven is to create the apocalypse. Needless to say, God does not have much use for people who think that blowing up God's creations is the way to win points with God. God is not watching and awarding points, but if God did favor anyone, why do some people think God would be pleased by murder and destruction?

There is a little trick that gets played on those who are deep believers in the biblical version of the Apocalypse. They can never know, at the moment of their own death, if they are dying alone, or with a small group around them,

OR... if the entire world is going up in flames or down in flood.

The truth is that each person suffers his or her OWN apocalypse. Death is the most intimate and solo act, and cannot be shared. The only "mistake" you can make as you die is to wish that your death is also the end of everything else, that if you are dying, it must also be the Apocalypse. What a cruel, self-centered view of the world for anyone who desires that!

Yes, you may ask a follow-up question.

97. Thank you. THEN HOW FAR WILL HUMAN
BEINGS ADVANCE? WHAT CHANGES WOULD
GOD LIKE TO SEE?

What makes you think that God "likes" to see
*any*thing you Earth people do? How come no one asks the
question, "Does God care what happens to us?"

Perhaps that question _has_ been asked in different
ways. For example, Question 24 asks how God wants to be
worshipped. If the answer is that God isn't concerned with
what YOU think of GOD, then perhaps you could put 2+2
together and figure out that GOD is not "thinking" about
YOU. Then there's Question 76 about whether you're here
to please God. God, as you learned there, is neither pleased
nor displeased with you. God is people-neutral. It's not
that God *should* or should *not* care about you. There's no
right or wrong here with God. It's that God is not a *person.*
Therefore, God does not have the *ability* to care. That's not
what God IS. God is the ENGINE of the cosmos, not the
foot on its accelerator.

That old V6 engine in your car is likely to continue
to do the things you expect of it longer if you treat it a
certain way, like changing its oil and not letting it run too
hot, and so on. Right? So, in the same sense that your
engine "likes" to be treated right, so God performs better
for Earth people when you do certain things. You could say
that there is a natural preference for particular behaviors.

That means you DO have to advance if, like past
societies on other planets, you want to continue your race
and preserve your home planet as long as possible.
Ultimately, if you survive long enough to have general
peace and prosperity on Earth, it will be because you have
learned how to communicate with each other. Only two
things will spur this advance over time. First, the
population of the Earth must be smaller. (See Question 233,

94

What should we do about overpopulation?) Second, the population that exists everywhere on the planet must realize that each tribe of people, each nationality (see Question 244 about Hitler) needs the other tribes and nationalities in order to survive.

A large-scale war is most likely to be the way you folks reduce the population, and that method, as you know, could spiral out of control into extinction of your species. But that's not what God has experienced on other planets like yours. In other words, Doomsday is not a foregone conclusion for you. Of course, if some of your religious wackos, your "Rapture" lovers, have their way, it's not only foretold; *they're* going to make sure it *happens.* Still, if you let them take care of their own extinction and leave the rest of the species alone, you could be onto something. Work together with people from all over the Earth who care about its resources and how long those resources will last. Work with Earthlings who see all other people as one of those resources, and not as an enemy. There doesn't have to be perfect fairness in how resources such as food and water are shared. There doesn't even have to be economic equity on Earth. But you will last longer if you make your world less unbalanced than it is today.

Now, of course, there's another way to interpret your question. Perhaps you want to know how human beings will evolve over the next few thousand years. You want to know what you'll look like and how smart you'll be and whether you'll sprout wings and fly, or something.

Well, you know what? God can't tell you. It's not that God *won't* tell you; God just can't because God has no idea how you'll turn out. Nothing exactly like you ever existed on any planet exactly like Earth in any solar system exactly like yours. Your brains may evolve to extraordinary capacity, or devolve from the pollutants in your air and water. You may lose unnecessary organs such as your appendix, or the shape of your skull (and thus, your face) might change to protect you from increased sun exposure. You may not *need* to fly because you'll have made such advanced robots, that you can attach one to yourself whenever you need to fly, and not worry about crashing into other people in the air because the robots will repel gravity. So, anything is possible if you survive long enough. Isn't that enough of a motivation to make peace instead of war?

98. OKAY, SO... *DOES* GOD CARE ABOUT ME?

No. No more than your car engine cares about you. Reread the last question. And that's your final follow-up. Let's move on. You there, in the back.

99. IS TIME TRAVEL POSSIBLE?

No, not like you see in the movies. It is the same "now" here where you are, and one mile from where you are, and one thousand miles from here, and one trillion miles away. To travel to a different time would require that it must be a different time in two adjacent places. Right now is the same instant in time everywhere, so even if you could be in two places at once, it would be the same time in both. It IS, however, possible to travel faster than the speed of light and to see the IMAGE of things that happened before, the same way you now see light that left distant stars eons ago. It is NOT possible to see the future, because it has not happened anywhere yet.

100. WHY DOES TIME SEEM TO CHANGE? WHEN WE ARE YOUNG, IT SEEMS TO GO SLOWLY, AND WHEN WE ARE OLD, IT SEEMS TO SPEED UP.

Time, of course, does not actually change. Only your perception has changed, and that's based on several things.

When you were younger, and people used record players, did you ever see someone place little things – dimes, small toys – on the turntable and turn it on at 33 1/3? The things don't move when the platter is just starting to spin or even when it reaches full speed. But change the speed to 45 rpm, and the things go flying off into space.

The brain of a child is like the disk drive of a new computer: lots of memory, most of it empty. It took many years to fill up your brain with data. When you were having all new experiences and learning language and art and science, your mind was filled with the wonder of each new acquisition of data, of memories. Now, the familiarity of most of your daily experiences takes the wonder out of most of your days. When you no longer pause to drink it all in, then the time seems to go faster. Each year seems to come around faster and faster, like that old turntable spinning faster and faster, until you feel like you are ready to go flying out into space.

Another factor is that the amount of stimulation you receive now is greater than when you were younger. You Earthlings have crafted a world in which the flow of information is virtually non-stop. The more the brain is forced to work, the faster time seems to go. Next time you're bored, take a look at how slowly the time passes.

101. WHY ISN'T THE WORLD PERFECT? *

Who says it isn't perfect? God understands why people may think things could be better, but many species of life on Earth are quite content. The Earth itself, as a geological entity, is turning out exactly as God expected. Keep in mind that God doesn't "expect" things the way a child does or a weather forecaster. "Expectation" for God means fulfillment of a natural process. (See Question 91, Does history repeat itself?) (See Question 91, Does history repeat itself?[2]) Other planets have experienced histories similar to Earth, and your results are pretty consistent with theirs.

The truth is that things on Earth are *not* perfect, though. God simply wanted to point out first that "perfect" is a relative term. Many things on Earth have not worked out as we would have projected. Take the level of pollution, for example. A certain amount of pollution is impossible to avoid, and all planets on which there is life have some by-products – both naturally and unnaturally occurring – that pollute the environment. Yet Earth people have raised pollution to a fine art. Some people seem to revel in the new and unique ways they find to ruin the air, water, and soil.

---

[2] Get it?

102. WHAT SURPRISES YOU MOST ABOUT HUMANS?

That you walk upright! When God first created Earth people, you did not walk upright. You dragged your knuckles and often crawled. Watch a baby get around. God has seen evolution on Earth and other planets make very dramatic changes in living things over time, but humans went from walking apelike to walking upright in a remarkably short period of time. That was a major surprise.

As for other surprises... oh, golly, where do we begin?

God is very surprised that you cheer and celebrate your men who are warriors, who *kill* other men. You call them heroes. But you scorn and ridicule your men who are lovers, especially those who *love* other men. You call them sick and degenerate. You value killing more than loving, yet you say that God is love. Indeed, all your books say you crave love and hate war, but almost nothing you do on a large scale supports that premise. At the very least, God is surprised at your inconsistency, and at the very worst, at your hypocrisy.

Every aspect of human thought has advanced dramatically over the past two millennia. Mathematicians understand concepts that no one even contemplated in biblical times. Science has discovered principles as basic as gravity and electricity, and as complex as atomic energy and the laser. Linguistics and music and graphic arts and economics have all become far more sophisticated. Yet when it comes to religion, humans still rely on the thoughts set down by people who believed that Earth was the center of the universe, that the Sun went around the Earth, that women were inferior and subservient to men, and that myrrh made a great gift. And these are the people whose version of creation you still believe? Amazing!

Another major surprise to God is the arrogance that has developed among Earth people. There are a few other planets where intelligent life thinks as highly of itself, but not many. Yet this arrogant nature defies all logic. Without question, people are the most intelligent beings on Earth, and the most capable of controlling their environment, but they are inferior in nearly all other respects to other beings, even comparing them just to other Earth inhabitants. For example, humans are not the fastest, or the strongest, or the tallest, or the most flexible. Without the aid of machines, you cannot fly and you cannot survive long underwater on a planet that is more than 75 percent covered with water. Humans can only see straight ahead, while many other animals have a much broader range of vision, not to mention more acute. Other animals have stronger senses of smell, and better hearing. No other animals kill for pleasure. As for beings on other planets, those that make laws for themselves are far less inclined to break those laws. And only Earth people have the hubris to believe they look like God and think like God, and to assume that, when they die, God will naturally want them by God's side, living in paradise forever.

It is surprising how powerful the sex drive is in most of you, so powerful that you will risk everything you hold dear for even a brief release, but that you then make laws forbidding you to do the very things your sex drives compel you to do, as if laws could stop what reason won't.

Finally, God is surprised by how superstitious humans are. Superstition is almost exclusively an Earthling trait. It is another manifestation of arrogance, because it implies that a person can change events or the nature of things just by existing or by saying or doing something

100

unrelated to the expected consequence. For example, why would walking under a ladder or breaking a mirror cause something bad to happen later? How could someone sitting in his or her living room saying that a baseball player is pitching a no-hitter jinx the pitcher and cause the other team to get a hit? Why would kneeling in church and repeating some traditional prayer help a sick person far away to get better? (See Question 162 about intercessory prayer.) Yet people believe all these superstitions and more. You didn't get *that* from God!

103. ARE PEOPLE INHERENTLY GOOD, INHERENTLY BAD, OR NEITHER?
Yes.

People are too diverse to be all *any*thing. Some people are born inherently good to parents who were born inherently bad. The diversity of creation and the effects of evolution guarantee that no trait will ever appear in ALL humans.

104. I WAS RAISED IN A TRADITIONAL RELIGION. I REALIZE THERE IS A "FORCE" THAT IS A PART OF ME. IT IS NOT PART OF MY PHYSICAL BODY OR MY CONSCIOUS MIND. I LIVE IN A THREE-DIMENSIONAL WORLD, BUT I SENSE ANOTHER FORCE BEYOND THOSE THREE DIMENSIONS. IT IS THERE. I HAVE EXPERIENCED ALTERED STATES OF CONSCIOUSNESS. WHAT IS THIS FORCE?

There are more than the four dimensions (the fourth dimension being time) that people know. Perhaps "dimension" is not the right word to describe what else there is, because that word specifically pertains to certain physical aspects of the cosmos, and the other "dimensions" are not physical in the same sense. You are on the cusp of evolution. In another 100 generations or so, Earth people may begin to understand and control forces beyond the physical, but for now, these additional forces are beyond your control or understanding. Rest assured, you are not in the clutch of some nameless power. There is no intelligence there, driving this force. You cannot control it, and it cannot control you. You can sense these forces are there, but that is as far as your experience will take you.

V. DEATH AND DYING
Or, WE'VE GOTTA GET OUT OF THIS PLACE IF IT'S THE LAST THING WE EVER DO

One woman wrote to us, "Dear God, have you met Fred? He passed your way at 9:15 p.m. on January 5, 2003. His wife Ruth would like to know. He was a member of UUCNH, Pittsburgh, Pennsylvania, USA, Planet Earth."

Death and dying are among the most prevalent topics that come up when people talk of God. There are two great unknowns with which people concern themselves: how did everything start, and how will it end? Not surprisingly, people want to know what comes next. We understand that life is but an interval. We just cannot know for a certainty what, if anything, comes after life ends. Thousands of books and articles have been written on this subject in every language. Much of what is written is based on faith. Some of it is based on the perceptions of people who had near-death experiences. But being *near* death is not the same thing as being dead, any more than being lightly asleep is the same thing as being awake. If that were true, our dreams would be much different, and much scarier.

Ruth's message begs the question, "Is there life after death?" That's just one of the Big Questions we will tackle in the Press Conference in this chapter.

103

105. A FRIEND SUGGESTED THAT WE ALL HAVE FREE WILL BEFORE WE COME TO EARTH, THAT IS, WE CHOOSE THE EXPERIENCES THAT WE WILL HAVE DURING THIS LIFE. I BOUGHT THAT. THEN HE SAID, "I BELIEVE THAT ALL OF THE MEN AND WOMEN WHO PERISHED ON 9/11 CHOSE THAT EXPERIENCE." SO, MY QUESTION IS, DO WE REALLY HAVE FREE WILL? ARE MATTERS OF OUR LIFE PREORDAINED? DO PEOPLE PERISH AND SUFFER BECAUSE THEY WILLED IT?

People *totally* have free will. God decides nothing about any individual, or even a group of individuals who just happen to be together in the same place at the same time. However... having free will is not the same thing as having total control. Those people who DO wish to suffer or even to die can generally do things to bring that about, but suffering and death come on untimely feet even to those who do not will it or wish it. Do not underestimate the power of chaos. Robert Burns got it right when he wrote, "The best-laid schemes o' mice an' men gang aft agley." Free will IS a gift, but it's still a good idea to look both ways when crossing the street.

106. WHY DOES AGING SCARE PEOPLE SO MUCH?

Because people cannot fully envision anything other than what they have experienced as a living Earth person, and aging brings them closer to ending that experience. Could you imagine yourself as, say, a donkey or a spider or a begonia or a surfboard? Of course not. You can barely empathize with other human beings. You have no way to know what it is to exist in any form other than as yourself, or indeed, not to exist at all. (See Question 19 about atheists.)

No matter what you believe about death, there is a fear that you might be wrong. It's the not knowing that sparks the fear. Only those who are completely certain of what happens next are calm about death, whether they believe firmly in a glorious afterlife or just as firmly that death is the absolute end of existence. But while some people are comfortable with death, almost no one is comfortable with dying. Except for condemned criminals, you cannot know the time or manner in which you will die, and that leaves room for so many undesirable possibilities. Young humans, whose bodies and minds work well and who have not yet felt the sting of years, think very little about the end of their existence. Once you begin to feel your age, you begin, too, to feel your mortality, the finiteness of your human form.

God does not feel there is any reason for you to be afraid of death. Read on.

107. WHY CAN'T DEATH BE PAINLESS?

The answer is that death IS painless, but dying hurts like a son-of-a-gun. God gives you great credit for not asking the usual question, which is why do things have to die. At least you have accepted that death is a natural part of life. Sometimes it is painless, and sometimes it is not. If God controlled the amount of pain, then God would also have to control all other aspects of living and dying, and believe me, you're better off the way things are.

Excuse me, but you don't have to jump up and down to get my attention. I take it you want to ask a follow-up question?

108. You bet I do. WHY *DOES* EVERYTHING GOD MAKES DIE? WHY DON'T PEOPLE LIVE FOREVER?

Well, would you prefer that it all lasted forever? In fact, would YOU want to last forever? And how does your family feel about that? (Just kidding!) Wouldn't that screw up the actuarial tables and pretty much put all the life insurance agents out of a job? Hmmm. Come to think of it...

Okay, no cheap shots at insurance agents. Let's work it from the top down. Your entire universe will not last forever. Therefore, nothing in it can last forever. So first, for something to BE infinite, it must exist in an infinite universe. If the universe were to last forever, would that mean that <u>all</u> its components must also last? Or could some components die? You ask why *everything* dies, but you did not indicate whether you think *everything* should survive, or only *some* things. Since the amount of matter in the universe (but not the cosmos) is finite, some things must end for new things to be created. And so it is on Earth. If nothing ever died, eventually you would reach a point where nothing new could be sustained.

Should things last forever? (See Question 88, Why does God treat old people so badly?) Is longevity the only measure of value? What about the quality of a thing's existence? (See Question 79, What is the meaning of life?) Of course, you would say that the quality of a person's existence is different from that of a fish or an amoeba or any other living thing, but is that necessarily true, or is that another case of human hubris?

109. IS IT FAIR YOU LIVE FOREVER, GOD, WHILE WE YOUR CHILDREN PERISH? WHY, CREATOR, ENDLESSLY DESTROY YOUR OWN CREATION?

You don't think it's fair that God gets to go on forever and you don't? Perhaps not, but that's the way it is for everything in the cosmos. You can't equate yourself or anything you know with God. You and God are nothing alike. You have more in common with rocks and air than you do with God. (See the previous question about things lasting forever.)

God does not destroy anything, nor does God prevent its destruction. Change is the only possibility that exists. Change is inevitable, but it is also desirable. If nothing ever changed from the moment of its creation, there would be no life, no Earth, no people. The price you pay for the good things that come from change is that things will not stop changing just because you like them best a certain way. Embrace change, for all that is good in life comes from it.

110. WHAT IS DEATH?

Before I give you God's answer to that excellent question, let me take a poll. How many of you are afraid of death? Raise your hand if you are afraid of death. Most of you. But why?

Hold out your hand, palm down. With your palm still facing down, make a fist, and then turn it over. Now, before you open your fingers, tell me... are you afraid of what is in there? Of course you're not, because unless you cheated, there is nothing in your hand, and you should not be afraid of nothing. Death is nothing, absolutely nothing. Therefore, there is no more reason to be afraid of death than to be afraid of the nothing in your hand.

How can I prove that death IS nothing? We can all agree that death is the opposite of life, right? What is dead is completely not alive, and what is alive is completely not dead. There is no middle ground, so they are total opposites. So, after you stop being alive, you are dead, right? What about BEFORE you were alive? That must also be death! Are you afraid of the time before you were alive? Of course not! So, life is an interval between deaths. But are these two deaths *equal?* First you are not alive, then you are, and then you are not again. So the question is, does the act of being alive, for even an instant, change the nature of the second not-alive period? The simple answer is, NO. Because nothingness is always the same. You cannot have two different kinds of nothing.

You should not fear death. You should not WANT death, either, but don't fear it. You were nothing before you were born, and that wasn't so bad, was it? One of the very best treatments of this subject was in the film "The Neverending Story." Did you see that? I recommend it highly as an allegory on death.

Of course, if death is the opposite of life, and death is nothing, then that begs the inevitable question, what is life? Life... is a fiction. You are the figment of a cosmic imagination. So are your house, your car, your pets, and your ideas. Is that too hard to take? Good, because it is a lie, though an intriguing one. I mean, what if you and everything you perceive were just someone else's fanciful, HIGHLY detailed imagination? Isn't that, when you come right down to it, what traditional religions think God is – someone who just dreams things up and makes them happen a certain way? But you see, life is not the ONLY opposite of nothing. Every THING in the universe – every mountain, every rock, every speck of dust, every molecule – is also the opposite of nothing. All life – human life and plant life – is just a different state of being a thing. You, a living being, are not fundamentally different from a rock. When you die, your body will return to this other state of being, and your thoughts will simply stop.

The question we prefer to answer is not "what is life," but "what are you?" You are the product of every life that came before you. Every person who ever lived is in you. Every thought they had, every memory, every little physical change, has made you what you are. When you are no longer alive, you will still be here in every person who comes after you. You ARE your memory; when your memory is gone, even if your body is still alive, you are no longer you. As you contemplate this connection between yourself and all people, try hard not to think about the humans who invent the challenges on "Fear Factor."

111. WHY DO ALL LIFE FORMS FIGHT DEATH AND STRUGGLE TO STAY ALIVE, PARTICULARLY PEOPLE WHO BELIEVE THAT DEATH WILL BRING UNION WITH GOD?

Death is the end. There is no union with God, at least not in any conscious way. There is no soul that escapes and outlasts the body. The problem is that "life" is just that – for the living. You can't be the opposite of alive and still be alive, at least not in the sense that you humans think of life.

You say that all life forms fight death. That's really not true. Very few life forms struggle for life. Many of them struggle for good health, but that's not the same thing as struggling to avoid death. Consider a plant that turns its leaves to the sun or spreads its roots to reach for water. The plant has no notion of its own existence, and so it has no notion that failure to do these things might end its existence. The plant "knows" only the goodness of life, but nothing about death.

However, we have noticed that many people who expect an afterlife and who expect to be in "union" with God are quite content with their impending death, while others seem frightened and will put up with almost anything to stay alive. We cannot explain that paradox. Maybe deep inside, they *do* know that death is the end.

112. WHY DO PEOPLE DIE SEEMINGLY BEFORE THEIR TIME? *

They don't. They die when it is exactly their time. We're not talking about "fate" here. There is no predetermination, no one pulling the strings to make people die at a certain time in a certain place. A life is just a life. The duration of that life is what it is. Do not think that it must be longer, for that is like playing the slot machines, always thinking that the next spin will be the right one. You may not be ready to let someone leave your life, but that is not the same thing as a life cut short.

Accidental death is traumatic, and there's no question that the person who dies in an accident would otherwise have lived longer and done more things with their life. Perhaps they died before they could marry and raise a family. Perhaps they would have done something else important with their life. Or... perhaps they would have lost their temper the very next day and hurt someone else, or stepped off the curb at the wrong time and caused an accident, or suffered terribly with a disease in just a few years. Do not dwell on the might-have-been. There is nothing but grief and regret there. Celebrate the life that was, for that is now a complete life, no matter how long.

113. IS THERE LIFE AFTER DEATH?

No. We know that will disappoint many of you. We understand why you would prefer a different answer, but we don't want to give you false hope. Death is the end. The problem is that "life" is just that – for the living. You can't be the opposite of alive and still be alive, at least not in the sense that you humans think of life. Life is a different experience for each living thing. For example, plants have no soul, but they are no less alive than you. When a plant dies, should it still be alive in some other form? You can't imagine what form that would be, can you? So, in the minds of many humans who believe in life after death, they are actually thinking only of human life, or maybe their pets, and God does not place a higher value on one creation than another. Since plants have no thoughts, no soul, people don't think of an afterlife for plants or lower animal species. But why? Should God preserve only the soul? Once again, the beliefs of people are tainted with arrogance and self-importance.

You should also consider – would you *really* want another life after this one? What if it were not the cushy eternal life everyone hopes they have earned? No, I'm not talking about hell. That's a no-brainer. But what if you could make it to heaven and it wasn't what you thought? The classic idea of heaven sounds great! Who wouldn't like peace and happiness and total satisfaction forever? Well, don't be so sure.

No person has just one spirit. You change dramatically in the course of your life. The attitudes and sensibilities of your 70's are not the same as those of your 40's or 20's or teens. Which attitudes would you take with you to eternity? Those you possess at your death? That's usually the moment of greatest anguish, both physical and mental. Not a good spirit to have forever. What about the spirit of your teens? Whoa! Not everyone thinks that's such a good idea? What's the matter? Not so enamored of spending eternity with a bunch of hormonal teenagers? So, would you get to choose which edition of yourself to be in heaven? Of all the notions espoused by established religions, this concept of eternal life is the most troubling. See the next question, too.

We are bemused that you want so desperately to believe in an afterlife. When you insist that the life you have is just the beginning, you are, in effect, being ungrateful for your life, or at least being greedy for more. What's wrong with what you have? Life itself is incredibly complex, and the fact you are a living person should be enough of a "gift" from God. Yet some of you are never satisfied. You want more. And not just a little more... you want eternal life. You want peace and joy forever. You want to be able to look down upon the loved ones you leave behind and help them through troubled times. In other words, you want to be God, or at least God Junior. You're barking up the wrong tree, or as we like to say, "charging the wrong particle." Your life will take on new meaning and new joy if you recognize it for what it is, not the beginning, but the whole enchilada, the entire gift you get. Therefore, you should treasure it; make it good and strong and worthwhile. If you really want to help your loved ones, do it now while you still can. Do not selfishly rely on an afterlife as the time you'll get it all done.

You can put this knowledge about death to good use. Next time you have to spell "cemetery," remember that there is nothing but "ease" (e's) in a cemetery.

114. Jeremiah, I would like to ask a follow-up question about death. CAN OUR LOVED ONES SEE US IN SOME WAY AFTER THEY DIE?

The answer is no, and you should be mighty glad. Would you really want all your ancestors to be able to see you? Sure, there are times you do things of which you are proud, and it's nice to think that they could see you and share in your joy. But you also do things that might not make them so proud. Do you think that they'd just look away at those times, so they would not be embarrassed? Well, if you think dead people can feel joy and shame, then I guess you think the afterlife is pretty much the same as *this* life, but with fewer good restaurants.

How can heaven be a place of eternal bliss if you can still feel all the human emotions of sorrow and fear and embarrassment? What's appealing about that? And it is no more appealing if you CAN'T feel those things, if you are just a bland, emotionless soul. You should take comfort in knowing that there is no afterlife, no one secretly watching your every move. When you are alone, you are truly, completely alone. Nothing in the universe, indeed, not even the universe itself, is spying on you.

115. Excuse me, but I have to follow up again. SO I WILL NEVER SEE MY DEAR DEPARTED MOTHER/UNCLE/SPOUSE/FRIEND AGAIN?

No, you won't. At least not after you yourself die. Even God cannot make something that no longer exists, exist again. To be dead is to be no longer alive. They are incompatible states of existence.

But here's the good news... God gave you senses and memory and sleep and dreams. That's all you need. While you are alive, you can see and hear and feel all of those people you miss. In fact, you don't even have to wait until they are dead. You can conjure them up and enjoy remembering them. If you can do that while they are alive but not with you, then you can also do it when they are gone forever.

116. HOW CAN I GET TO HEAVEN?

You don't have to worry about that. Ha! That's just a little Almighty humor there.

Look, heaven's not what you think. It's not a place you can "get to," like climbing on some train. That only works in gospel songs. You can't buy a ticket to heaven by donating money to a church or by living a good clean life, or even by confessing all your sins and accepting God on your deathbed. It's not some destination for you after you *die*. It's where your mind goes every time you dream. And it goes there again just *before* you die, not after. That's why people who are revived near death think they saw heaven. They *did* see heaven, and then they had their own living body to which to return. But if their body dies, then their mind is stuck in heaven, and it can never come back. Where dreams go... the fifth dimension... that's heaven. There's nothing real in heaven, only things that *were* real or which your imagination conjured up. That's why heaven and hell are the same thing. You can be in heaven one minute and hell the next. Of course, "minutes" don't actually mean anything, because time is not part of that dimension. And people you see there are not physically there. *Your* heaven is only *your* heaven. You can't invite anyone else in.

117. IS THERE A PLACE CALLED HELL? IF SO, WHAT IS IT LIKE?

No one seems to have noticed that life on Earth is no bed of roses for anyone. This life you have is really an experimental form of hell. Think about it. If you were God and you were creating Paradise, would you put mosquitoes and gnats there? For the vast majority of people in your world, there is hunger, random death, great pain, and emotional misery. Yes, there is joy and love, but the possibility of those things just makes the suffering that much greater. Think of the poor cow or camel that is so often beset with flies and bugs in their eyes and nose that they no longer even bother to swat at them. If that's not hell, what is?

If you want to get out of hell, you have only to work to make Earth better. God has already provided all the resources to you that God is *ever* going to provide. No one is forcing you to live in hell.

118. IS THERE PURGATORY, A PLACE WHERE DEAD SOULS ARE JUDGED?

No, that would be disgusting! Who wants to be around all those dead people?

No, really, there is no heaven or hell after death. There's no soul that floats invisibly away. The purgatory is in the minds of the living who knew the person. THEY do the judging. No matter how many nice things they say about the deceased, they're weighing the evidence silently in their minds.

119. I just have to follow up on that. IF THERE IS NO HEAVEN OR HELL, WHAT IS THE MOTIVATION FOR PEOPLE TO BE GOOD IN THIS LIFE?

Why must there be a "reward" for good behavior or "punishment" for bad in order for people to do the right thing? By this reasoning, once good people get to heaven, they no longer have any reason to behave themselves, and heaven should be full of obnoxious, ill-behaved angels, while hell should be full of souls who are goody-goodies trying for a "promotion."

The trouble with popular notions of heaven and hell is that they make God out to be pretty narrow-minded about God's creations. It would appear hell exists so that God can get rid of those people (created by God) who just didn't work out so well. Why do folks think that God would create a universe in which something that was bad would have to suffer through eternity? What does that say about the quality of God's work? Do they feel God runs the whole factory except for Quality Control?

Another problem with these notions is that God is depicted as being rather like a loan shark who gleefully lets people get themselves deeper and deeper in debt, until suddenly repayment is demanded "or else." It's as if God were saying, "Okay, I let you misbehave. *Now* you must *pay!*" The devil is seen as little more than a thug, and banishment to hell is the equivalent of the deliberately broken kneecap.

So many people seem to think that Earth is some gigantic Pavlovian experiment, with God as Pavlov and people as the dogs! That if they do the wrong thing, God will give their lives the equivalent of an electric shock. They think they WILL BE punished, if not in this life, then in the next one. Well, I hate to tell those folks, but God is not some kind of behavioral modification therapist.

Obviously, their fear is that anyone who is not afraid of God will not feel guilt, and therefore will be amoral or worse, immoral. Yet because there is no afterlife, there can be neither punishment for evil deeds nor reward for good ones. heaven – the reward – and hell – the punishment – exist only on Earth, in life. Therefore, you make your own heaven or hell. There is no room for evil, for hurting others, for committing, in other words, amoral or immoral acts that cause hurt to others. You cannot sin with impunity, for there can be no deathbed or jail-cell conversions to save you. If you steal, or kill, or cheat on your spouse, you create your own hell from which escape is difficult. In today's lingo, you might call it "virtual hell."

God does not intervene in the patterns of anyone's life or the other aspects of existence. That fact worries some people, who say that if God is indifferent to evil, then people who no longer fear retribution from God will go wild and visit tremendous evil upon the Earth. God supposes that *could* happen, but that has not been the experience on other planets on which the beings have not created for themselves a fearful version of God.

The worst evil on Earth comes from terrorists. It is the worst evil because it not only destroys innocent people and other animals, but also because it destroys the lives of millions of people who are *not* killed, but "merely" tormented. In almost every case, the terrorist feels justified in his or her actions and, far from fearing *retribution* from God, actually expects praise and permanent life in heaven. Remove that expectation, and many terrorists would realize that they are not going to be *rewarded* for their behavior. They are just going to be *dead.*

So, the true result of recognizing that God will not dole out rewards and retribution is actually GREATER motivation to live a good, moral life.

120

120. I have a follow-up. SHOULDN'T PEOPLE BE
AFRAID THAT THEY MIGHT GO TO HELL IF THEY
ARE EVIL OR DON'T WORSHIP GOD?
Obviously, people who don't believe in hell will not
be afraid. And just as obviously, if people believe in hell,
they are going to have real fear of retribution. The problem
is that most evil people don't see themselves that way. It's
always the *other* guy who's going to hell.

The most evil people, as we just said in the previous
question, are terrorists. Even THEY do not fear going to
hell for their heinous acts. But they might be less inclined
to be so evil if they did not expect to be rewarded.

In truth, you Earthlings have nothing to fear from
God. As we said above, God is not a behavioral
modification therapist, giving you electric shocks when you
stray down the wrong path. Bad things may happen to you,
but not because some all-powerful being decided they
should happen. The same with the good things you enjoy.
Those fortunate aspects of your life come about from being
a good, moral person, hard working and honest. They are
NOT the bounty from some Santa-Claus-like God who sees
you when you're sleeping and knows if you've been bad or
good, and then bestows rewards on you accordingly.

121. DO WE KNOW PEOPLE FROM PAST LIVES?
No, not in the way you know people in your current
life, and certainly not in the Bridey Murphy sense of
remembering a previous life you lived. People do not get
reincarnated. God is very big on recycling, but only energy
and matter, not souls. Pieces of your ancestors —the
experiences from which they learned, their physical
structure, their attitudes towards the world – reside within
you and help make you what you are today.

122. ARE THERE GHOSTS?
No.

123. Wait a minute! I have to follow up, Jeremiah. A GREAT MANY PEOPLE, INCLUDING LOTS OF HONEST, SINCERE PEOPLE, HAVE SEEN GHOSTS OR APPARITIONS. IF THERE ARE NO GHOSTS, WHAT DID THEY SEE? WERE THEY LYING?
They were not lying, but misled. What you mean when you say "ghost" is the visible spirit of a dead person, a previous inhabitant of Earth. To believe in such ghosts, you must believe first that the soul of a person lives on after death AND that these souls can, with no real body, make themselves appear in body-like form. But, as we have said previously, death is the end; there is no soul that lives on with the memories and personality of the deceased. Therefore, such ghosts are not possible, which brings us to the question of what DO people see.

The apparitions you or your fellow Earthlings see are projections of mischievous extra-terrestrials. That's right... aliens. (See Question 66 about intelligent beings from other planets.) Once in a while, they like to mess with your heads. It's not their most endearing quality.

124. WHERE IS THE HOPE FOR THOSE WHO KNOW THAT LOVE IS STRONGER THAN DEATH, WHEN DEATH SEPARATES THOSE WHO LOVE EACH OTHER?

Where is the *hope*? Is life hopeless unless all the things you treasure in life just keep going even after you die? Is love meaningless? The good news is that you will never feel disappointed by what happens after you're dead because, well, you won't feel *any*thing after you're dead.

Love is one of the things that makes life joyful, meaningful, and, for some, bearable. Death is not an extension of life. The things that are important in life have no meaning at all when life is gone. But why treat that as *bad* news? Those who focus on an afterlife are missing so much of what is good and exciting in the life they *have*.

One reason life can be wonderful is that it has such things as love in it. That makes life different from death. God does not blame you for wishing you could keep all the good things of life with you forever. That's very understandable. It's those things you have now that are familiar to you, that are comfortable. When you're told that death doesn't have those same things, there's a sense of impending loss. God's take on that is... Big Whoop. Get over it.

Oh, you don't think it's fair that God gets to go on forever and you don't? Well, you better get over that, too. You can't equate yourself with God. You and God are nothing alike. You have more in common with a toadstool or a firefly than you do with God. And compared to your life, toadstools and fireflies aren't doing so well. They have very short and often violent lives. So, what are *you* complaining about?

You want hope? Then hope for a life full of love given and received. Hope that the people you love have the same. Hope that they and you get lots of good time together, without hunger or sickness or pain to separate you. And don't just *hope*, but do something about it to make it so. Then you will find even greater love on Earth.

125. WHY IN THE WORLD DOES GOD MAKE THE LIFESPAN OF DOGS SO SHORT? THAT'S A VERY BAD DECISION!

God did not evaluate each creature and assign a general lifespan to each, like some actuary or personnel director run amok. God did not even create each species of animal or plant independently. Evolution does that. It's nice that you feel dogs should live longer. Perhaps 300-year-old tortoises feel the same way about humans.

VI. RELIGION
Or, YOU CAN'T TEACH AN OLD GOD NEW TRICKS

There are three "professions" that probably predate all others among Earthlings: people who provide sexual services for others, people who govern and lead others, and people who make it their business to tell others what to think and how to explain the mysteries of life.

No other aspect of modern life generates more hatred, animosity, and violence than the different views of God and nature and life collectively called "religions." Religion – faith, if you will – is also responsible for some of the greatest joys in life. People find comfort in the easy river of religious thought and doctrine, and they find community among people who share the same tenets of faith. Religion is the body of beliefs that we take "on faith," with scant, if any, evidence to support our views. Thus, even atheism is a "religion," in that atheists take on faith their own explanation of how life began and what, if anything, steers the course of all life and all creation. Religion is a balm to some, a poison to others. It is the most often debated and the least understood facet of human existence, and so, of course, it generates some of the most poignant, complex, and important questions to God.

126. ARE YOU ALSO THE PRESS SECRETARY FOR JESUS AND THE HOLY SPIRIT?
No. Jesus already has enough people who THINK they speak for him.

125

127. YOUR BOSS IS KNOWN BY MANY NAMES AND WORSHIPPED WITH MANY DIFFERENT RITUALS. IS THERE A NAME GOD LIKES BEST AND A RITUAL THAT IS HIGHLY EXPRESSIVE OF GOD'S NATURE?

God is "God." Or Jahweh. Or Allah. Or G*d. Or Dieu. Or Gravity. Or Energy. Or Time. Or Everything. How can you give a name to that which is not a thing or a person or even an idea? God does not care about *anything*, much less what word or name you use to invoke God. God is not listening. God does not have the *ability* to listen or to care. God is not a radio talk show host with an infinite number of call-in lines.

Is there a ritual expressive of God's nature? Yes, but it's not what _you_ think of as a ritual. It is the ritual of existence, the dance of all things in harmony and in chaos. The ritual that best expresses God is the way things change. Study an old person's face or hands. Watch a butterfly flaps its wings. Catch the snow on your tongue. It changes. Throw a leaf into the wind. Bury a rock in the sand. All these things express God.

128. HOW DOES GOD FEEL ABOUT THE CRITICISM AND PARODIES OF RELIGION AND OF GOD BY MONTY PYTHON, MEL BROOKS, AND OTHERS?

It is not possible to offend God. If it *were* possible, mere words would not do it. The only way to show disrespect to God is in showing disrespect to God's creations: the environment, the animals, the plants, and, of course, other people. And anyway, if God hated cheap shots and bad jokes, would I still be the Press Secretary?

129. I HAVE WONDERED IF GOD HAS A SUPPORT
OFFICE! WE PORTRAY ANGELS AS DOING GOD'S
WORK IN OUR REALM. ARE THERE "AGENTS" WE
CAN ENLIST TO FACILITATE OUR EFFORTS ON
EARTH?

No, there are no "hired guns" out there just waiting
for your call so they can come to your rescue. (See Question
153, Are there angels?) Can you imagine the personnel
nightmares we'd have keeping track of these angels you
dream of? We just don't have the staff.

So, as to the first part of your question, the obvious
answer is Yes, God has a support office.   What am I?
Chopped light-years?   It's smaller than the one
pictured on the TV series "The West Wing." God does not
need nearly as many helpers as you'd think.   There's
actually just a handful of us. We have an archivist, of
course, to try to keep track of things like which universe is
expanding and which is *collapsing.*   Then there's me,
"Jeremiah Spin Control" as I am known. (By the way, "spin"
has a whole different meaning from our perspective.) We
have a small Science Committee that notes any changes in
the physics and chemistry of the cosmos, looking for any
Lawbreakers.   There are, I think, six members of the
Committee,   and   they   are   *incredibly*   busy   taking
measurements and looking things up. Finally, there's the
Living Things Control Officer (LTCO). You don't want to
know *their* job.

By the way, none of us on the Support Staff are
people. You are just imagining that I look like a human
being because that's what you need to see.

The ancient Greeks and Romans and other cultures
that developed a mythology with many different gods kind
of got this idea of a Support Staff, but they imagined the
staff as separate "gods," which is not right. There is only

127

one God, manifest in everything you observe in your world. But God is not manifest in your feelings. Those are all yours. You don't need a Venus to get by. (See Question 29 about other gods.)

130. WHY SHOULD I BELIEVE IN GOD? WHAT EVIDENCE IS THERE THAT GOD EXISTS?

There is no reason for you to believe in God. There is also no reason NOT to believe. No matter whether you believe there is a God or not, your belief is founded on FAITH. Most people say that an atheist lacks faith. That's simply not true. "Faith" is any belief that is based on an individual's perception when hard evidence is missing. No one can prove to the atheist that there is a God. No one can prove to the theist that there is not.

So, it's not important what you believe. What is important is what you DO with your belief. If your faith in God or faith that there is no God leads you to be a better person, to make the most of your life, and to enjoy your life, then HOW you think of God and IF you think of God are irrelevant. No one, not even God, should judge you on your thoughts. I would refer you to Question 13 about God's existence, and I see you have a follow-up question.

131. Right. IS IT OKAY NOT TO BELIEVE IN GOD?

God does not judge you on your thoughts. As we just said in the last question, you should be judged only on what you *do* with your beliefs, your thoughts.

So, you ask, is it okay not to believe in God. The truth is that *everything* is okay with God. If you were all powerful and everywhere at once, how could anything happen that was NOT okay with you? There are only three possibilities if you are God:

1) You are God, and you have the ability to make things occur or not occur. You *could* prevent something bad from occurring. In other words, everything that occurs was controlled by you, and must, therefore, be exactly what you planned it to be. Or,

2) You have the ability to control things, to prevent bad things, but you choose not to do so sometimes. Since you *chose* not to interfere to change something, then you must be okay with your choice. If you're NOT okay with what you chose to do in spite of all your power, then you are not a very good omnipotent being, and if mere humans can figure out that you're not so good, then you're no longer omnipotent. Or,

3) You are NOT able to prevent bad things from occurring. What does that say about your powers? Apparently, you're NOT all powerful, are you?

The truth is that God is not what you think God is. No human being understands God. God is beyond the understanding of anything in the cosmos. You will come closer to understanding God if you stop believing in the God of your fathers and mothers. Everything is okay with God, because... everything IS God.

129

132. I AM CONFIDENT THAT THERE IS NOT A
GOD AND THAT HUMANS MAKE THIS STUFF UP
FOR VARIOUS REASONS. I AM RESPECTFUL OF
THIS EARTH, MY FELLOW PEOPLE, AND THE
INTERDEPENDENT WEB OF ALL EXISTENCE.
WHY DO CHURCHES EXIST, WITH ALL THEIR
MONEY, POWER AND RULES, TO SELL THE IDEA
THAT GOD EXISTS AND CAN HELP?

God is glad you are so confident that there is no
God. You really don't have to believe in God to be a good
person. (See Questions 130 and 131 above.)

You say you are respectful of this planet, and that
would be music to God's ears if God had ears. Too many
people worship God while desecrating and destroying God's
work, so God does not need you to believe there is a God as
long as you believe in and honor what has been created,
including yourself.

God did not create the churches you so easily
criticize. Money and power and rules are creations of
people, not of God. God does not talk to people and direct
them what to do in God's name. God has no ego and
doesn't need or want publicity. Anyone who says they
speak for God is mistaken. Except for me, of course.

133. WHAT ARE SOME ORIGINS OF FAITH?

Normally, we don't like to answer questions that scientists and sociologists are studying, mostly because we find the answers *they* come up with so darned entertaining! Like that whole "sun-moves-around-the-Earth" thing. We were kind of disappointed when you finally figured it out. However, this question is intriguing, so God has agreed to help you understand.

Almost every form of intelligent life in the cosmos has developed some sort of answer to the Big Questions: How did we get here? What happens when we die? And in almost every case, the reason they even asked these questions was the same: abject fear. Here's an example.

On the planet Blorph in the Gknisfudn Galaxy, two very primitive beings – equivalent, I suppose, to "men" here on Earth – were out gathering food for their tribe. Suddenly, a large rock fell on the first being, who was called Rrrrumsfeld because of the sound he made in his sleep. The other being, named Mupp, saw the rock fall on Rrrrumsfeld, completely covering the poor fellow and, needless to say, killing him. Mupp had never seen another tribe member simply disappear, and in an effort to comprehend what had occurred, ended up inventing a complicated, comprehensive, and completely erroneous explanation for what happened to Rrrrumsfeld, why it happened, and where Rrrrumsfeld was now. Beings on Blorph to this day still worship Mupp as a great prophet, accepting on faith his philosophy of life. They are known as Muppets, and they are rather constantly at war with the followers of another equally mistaken prophet named Nosir, who, of course, are called Nosirees.

To take something "on faith" is to believe it in the absence of any hard evidence. If you had absolute proof about what happens when you die, you would not need faith, and virtually every religion on Earth would instantly go out of business, which, of course, is reason enough for established religions to keep making up whoppers that you can never prove or disprove.

134. WHAT IS THE DIFFERENCE BETWEEN A CULT AND A RELIGION?

Basically, just longevity. Every one of today's religions started off as a "cult" to people in the societies where they were born. Cults eventually gain legitimacy simply by surviving. Any group that fails to last more than 100 years or so is generally relegated to "cult" status. This benchmark is good news for anyone who wants to be considered a prophet someday by lots of people, but no one ever achieves prophet status in their own lifetime, except, perhaps, in the eyes of a few disciples. Your Bible's "New Testament" is something of a primer on how to achieve lasting status. Unfortunately, usually you have to be killed or at least grossly insulted.

135. WHAT IS TRUTH?

Do you mean, what things happen to be true, or do you want to know the definition of "truth?" Actually, it pretty much doesn't matter which question you ask, the answer is the same: it is beyond your knowing. We cannot tell you what is true, in part because truth is different in each place and for each thing. What is true on Earth may not be true elsewhere in the cosmos. What is true for you may not be true for someone else. The One Great Truth is Change. That, and the fact that the song "MacArthur Park" is reviled everywhere in the cosmos.

136. GOD'S BOOKS – THE BIBLE, TORAH AND KORAN – THAT ARE EASILY MISUNDERSTOOD, HAVE RESULTED IN CHRISTIANITY, JUDAISM, AND ISLAM HAVING CAUSED MORE WOE IN THE WORLD THAN ANYTHING ELSE. WHAT DEFENSE DOES GOD HAVE?

Where did you get the idea that these are God's books? Do you really think that God would write three different books and give them to different groups of people? No God could be that underhanded or cruel. In fact, everyone agrees that God would not write *three* such books, which is why each group thinks they have the only authentic manuscript.

Have you noticed how easily someone can spread misinformation on the Internet? Some clever but unethical wacko makes up some story, puts it out on the Internet, and within a few days, it's all over the world and 95 percent of the people who receive it think it's true. Well, I hate to say it, but there have always been people like that willing to dupe their fellow citizens for fun or for some advantage. The books you cited in this question are the "urban legends" of their time. Like all urban legends and hoaxes, they *seem* to make sense, to have enough credibility that readers let down their guard and accept it as truth. God has no defense because God committed no OFFENSE. The Bible, the Torah, and the Koran were not written by God.

Having said that, let me say that God does not agree that Christianity, Judaism, and Islam are inherently evil. Rather, we think that a significant percentage of ALL PEOPLE is inherently evil, and evil people gravitate towards philosophies that they can distort to their aims. They use religion to *legitimate* their evil nature. What is that human saying? "Guns don't kill people. People kill people?" We feel the same way about religion. What *should*

133

we think? No religion's got it right, but they all _think_ they do.

137. You know what my follow-up is, don't you? OKAY, SO WHO WROTE THE BIBLE?

I figured you'd ask that. Isn't it interesting how so many people believe all this really cool stuff happened thousands of years ago, and then it just stopped? You'd think they'd be a lot more disappointed.

Well, it sure wasn't God. If God wanted to give you a message, it would not be written in some ancient language open to so many different interpretations and partially hidden next to the Dead Sea. Why would God, with all the power of the universe, do something so important as to reveal – allegedly – the secrets of creation and the laws God wants you all to obey, and then leave it to chance that you'd ever find it?

_No_body actually _wrote_ the Bible. People told stories to their children and their neighbors, who then told those same stories, with their own slight revisions, to _their_ children and neighbors. After just a few generations, long before even one percent of Earth people knew how to read and write, the stories bore only a passing resemblance to the original. (Much like the game of "telephone" that many young humans like to play.) Eventually, someone who _could_ read and write decided to record one or more stories, until the collection you call the Bible was born. But you could hardly say these scribes were the authors. The Bible and other books like it were written by hundreds or even thousands of people over many, many generations. They are no closer to fact than a fairy tale.

138. WHY ARE THERE SO MANY RELIGIONS, AND HOW DO WE KNOW WHICH ONE TO BELIEVE IN AND FOLLOW?

The Rev. Sarah Stewart, a Unitarian Universalist minister, said that what she likes about UUism is that it actually encourages people to be themselves and to hold *diverse* thoughts, while other churches want individuals to accept ONE truth, to be more alike. God thought this was a good answer. God created diversity on Earth. God created every place on Earth to be different. Most of the planet is covered with water, but some of it is covered with dry desert, and some with harsh rocks, and some with green jungles. Some of the Earth is cold and unfriendly to life, and some is hot and just as unfriendly. God created different minerals and substances. God created millions of different species of life: plants and animals and people. And God created people of different colors, different sizes and shapes, different likes and dislikes. How can *any*one look at this diversity and believe that God wants everyone to THINK the same, to ACT the same, to BE the same? God has no favorite people and no favorite religious denomination, but you can be sure that God thinks very highly of Unitarians, Universalists, Taoists, Buddhists, and anyone else who respects diversity and the environment God created.

This diversity also explains, by the way, why there are so *many* religions. From the very beginning of human consciousness, people have tried to fathom how they got here, what life is about, and answers to all the questions we've dealt with today. Until the last 200 years or so, people were never subjected to more than one set of answers because there was no mass communications, most people could not read anyway, and they almost never traveled beyond a 25-mile radius from their home. So, of course, a person who is born in the mountains of Tibet will produce a different explanation for the world than one who

135

is born in a jungle or a desert. God does not interfere with the evolution of ideas any more than God interferes with the evolution of bodies. Diversity is God's greatest gift to the universe, and change – evolution – is its driving force.

God will not be drawn into any debate about which religion is "best," or even to comment on each denomination of each religion. That debate is a trap. Almost every religion admits that the "facts" about creation and life are unknowable, yet then proceeds to say that they have the only true and complete explanation. Billions of people on your planet have, literally, billions of ideas about how and why they exist, yet some religions manage to ignore all these inconvenient ideas in favor of just one dogma. As we said in answer to Question 136, no one religion has it all right. Most religions have part of it right, and a few managed the incredible feat of getting every single answer wrong.

139. Jeremiah, please may I follow up? IF, AS YOU SAY, MOST RELIGIONS ARE WRONG IN THEIR CORE BELIEFS, SHOULD THEY STOP WHAT THEY'RE DOING? SHOULD THERE BE JUST ONE RELIGION? WOULDN'T GOD'S JOB BE EASIER?

You might be surprised to learn that God is not concerned about religion one way or the other. It doesn't matter.

Look at it this way. There are dozens of so-called "organized" religions on Earth. Some are pretty similar to others, and some are broadly different. Suppose, just for the sake of argument, that one religion's explanations for creation and life and society are completely right. They nailed it! They looked at all the evidence from the past thousands of years, and they figured out how it all began and what it all means. Doesn't that mean that virtually every other religious belief is wrong? Of course it means that! You can't have TWO correct explanations that don't match each other.

Okay, so if you can't have two or more correct religions on Earth, then the _best_ you can hope for is ONE religion that got it right. Well, there's not a heck of a big drop from ONE right to NONE right. And that's exactly what you've got. Not one religion on Earth has the whole story correct. Neither does science, though science is doing a whole lot better than theology.

But I digress. If no one on Earth fully understands how the cosmos works and what God is, then why shouldn't there be lots of different attempts made? Let people scurry around thinking about it, and trying out new answers.

The complete truth about the nature of all existence and the nature of God is BEYOND HUMAN UNDERSTANDING. No religion could ever fill in all the gaps. And you should be GLAD of that. Earthlings are not sufficiently evolved to be able to comprehend the magnitude and significance of the secrets of the cosmos. A little knowledge, as the Earth saying goes, is a dangerous thing.

Now, you ask if having a single religion with all the answers would make God's job easier. Easier than what? Is being God a "job?" 'Cause if it is, I think God will probably want to negotiate a new benefits package. What God does is not "work" as you think of it. God works in mysterious ways, indeed.

140. WE ALL KNOW JESUS WAS JEWISH AND
THAT HE CELEBRATED THE JEWISH TRADITION
OF PASSOVER THE NIGHT BEFORE HE WAS
CRUCIFIED. YET THE PEOPLE WHO FOLLOW
JESUS REJECT JEWISH TRADITIONS AND CALL
THEMSELVES CHRISTIANS. SO MY QUESTION IS,
IF JESUS WERE ALIVE TODAY, WHAT RELIGION
WOULD HE BE?

In Jesus' time, before the early Christians concocted
all the mythology that is so revered today, there was no
need to talk about one-God issues (the "Trinity") or
universal salvation. Jesus believed that people should be
allowed to be themselves, that they should have the freedom
to hold diverse thoughts. Jesus recognized something few
people in his day acknowledged: that God created diversity
on Earth. Jesus saw only a tiny fraction of the Earth, and so
did not perceive just *how* vast and diverse a place it already
was.

Yet even in the very small area where Jesus roamed,
he saw people living in dry desert and rocky highlands and
lush farms. And more than anything, he understood that
PEOPLE were not all the same, and that justice, equity, and
compassion were needed for everyone, including the ultra-
poor class of which he was a member. He recognized that
each person had inherent worth and was deserving of
dignity and acceptance. So today, Jesus would be called a
Unitarian-Universalist, and Jerry Falwell would call him a
fruitcake, or worse.

141. WAS JESUS REALLY THE SON OF GOD?

Yes and no. Mostly no. Don't you find it amusing the way many Christians think of God? They believe that God could just "point and click" and create Adam and Eve, but later, when God, the chauvinist male, wanted a son, he had to impregnate a teenager? What's up with that?! It makes no sense! God is not some kind of stud, just here to procreate one way or another. And God certainly doesn't multiply like some sexual organism.

Jesus was no more or less the "son" of God than any other man is. Every man and woman who ever lived on Earth has a real, biological father, Jesus included. Mary was not a virgin when she gave birth to Jesus, and she never said she was. That little fable was made up many years after she died. Remember... she was *married*, and Jewish marriages were to be consummated. She was a good mother, and she raised Jesus right, especially given how poor they were, and he grew up to have a very great understanding of goodness and fairness.

People who believe that Jesus was the son of God, sent to Earth to die for their sins, are really missing the mark. So many people think and act like they don't have to take any responsibility for their own actions, because they can be absolved of all guilt as long as they accept Jesus at any point before they die. What fool came up with that bright idea? It wasn't God, that's for sure.

You can't be a jerk your whole life – dishonest, or mean, or violent, or disrespectful of any of God's other creations – and just get that slate wiped clean because you mutter a few words or have some remorse or fear of damnation. God created life, but does not intervene. If you are bad OR good, you're still on your own. (See Question 77, Why do bad things happen to good people? and Question 119, What is the motivation for people to be good

140

in this life?) You must take personal responsibility for the quality of your life. No fair sloughing that one off on some teacher who's been dead for thousands of years.

And God wants you to know: Jesus is not coming back, folks. There have been and will be other men and women who understand goodness as well as Jesus. If you're waiting for Jesus to return, you're missing all the Christ-like people who walk among you today.

Let me guess. Now you want to know...

142. WHO ARE THESE CHRIST-LIKE PEOPLE TODAY?

You may be surprised at some of the people who share Jesus' more admirable traits. Of course, most of them are not famous. Among the names you would recognize and expect to see on such a list are Nelson Mandela, Ralph Nader, Aung San Suu Kyi, and Desmond Tutu. But you might be surprised to see Maya Angelou, Michael Jordan, and Susan Sarandon. They all shine for different reasons. And though, like Jesus Christ, none of them is perfect, they still have many qualities worth emulating. (Also see Question 199, Are there any people you don't like?)

143. HOW MANY "SAVIORS" ARE THERE IN GOD'S KINGDOM THAT YOU CAN FURNISH TO NEWLY DISCOVERED CIVILIZATIONS?

None. (And it's not a "*king*dom.")

141

144. WHO WAS RIGHT – JESUS CHRIST, BUDDHA, MUHAMMAD, OR SOMEONE ELSE?

You are really trying to get me in trouble with just about everyone on Earth, aren't you? As we said above, God will not be drawn into any debate about which religion is "best" or "right." Most religions, and most of the people whose teachings those religions follow, have much wisdom to impart. If you want a good life for yourself and the people about whom you care most, open your ears to ALL these teachers, but don't assume that any of them were infallible. No human ever achieved total understanding of God and the cosmos, and all of these men you named were human. (See the next question and Question 138 about the different faiths.)

145. HAS GOD SENT PROPHETS TO EARTH OR SPOKEN TO PEOPLE AND TOLD THEM WHAT TO SAY TO EVERYONE ELSE? IF SO, ARE THERE ANY PROPHETS ON EARTH TODAY?

Cool idea!

It seems like in the old days, some of the people you call "prophets" were just early versions of press secretaries, right? Oops, nope. Sorry. They told you what *they* thought, not what God told them to say. The same is true today; God does not talk to Earthlings or any other being, for that matter.

The early prophets tried to be philosophers, expounding on their own thoughts about the origins and destinies of Earth people. That's a very natural pursuit for a human. But these early humans did not have the developed language or literary skills to record their thoughts. So they told them to other people. As these "prophets" got older, their wacky ideas seemed to make more sense, seemed to carry the "wisdom of the ages." And so young people, boys mostly, would hear the philosophers and assume that their version of creation and human history is correct! It was many years before anything was written down, and in those years, many new words were created and added to the human lexicon, and the stories were no longer the same. By then, the stories were not just conjecture; they had taken on the proportions of *myth*. God has never sent prophets to Earth. God does not speak to Earthlings or to other beings in anything you would call "language." God will not send any prophets to Earth anytime in the future. That *ain't* God's *thing*. (See Question 142, Who is like Jesus today? Also see Question 164, What about minor prophets and founders of various faiths?)

146. DOES GOD EVER PUT IMAGES OF JESUS OR MARY OR ANY OTHER RELIGIOUS PERSON ON WALLS, IN FOOD, OR ANY OTHER PLACE PEOPLE MIGHT FIND IT?

Gee, you left out the Shroud of Turin! We are having trouble taking this question seriously, but since many Earthlings rejoice in believing it, we really don't want to ruin their fun, not to mention all the money that some places make from the tourism.

And what is it they believe? That God would toy with you by leaving tantalizingly vague clues about something or other. The problem is, many different religions recognize "signs from God." They then spend decades debating what the sign meant. That view depicts God as a gleeful misanthrope who sprinkles indecipherable graffiti all over just to drive people nuts. What possible good would come from God doing such a thing? Why would God want to mess with your head? Just what "message" do you think God is trying to send?

Don't you think that if God urgently needed to impart something *really important* to you all, that God would find a better way to do it than badly drawn pictures of Jesus or Mary? If you believe that God can do anything God wants to do, then you must believe that God could give you some very clear message. And don't go pointing to the Bible or the Koran. (See Question 136 on whether God wrote those books.) If God were able to publish books, God would print them in every language and not rely on your misguided interpreters to rework the words. And certainly, God would come out with a new, updated edition more often than every millennium. Heck, the way your planet is going, you could use daily briefings!

147. IT SEEMS AS IF THE HUMAN CONCEPTION OF GOD IS CHANGING. SHOULD IT CHANGE, AND IF SO, HOW SHOULD IT? WHAT SHOULD OUR CONCEPTION BE?

The human conception of everything is changing, and changing constantly. How could a society be the same today as it was less than 20 years ago, before Lean Cuisine®, MTV, and Powerball®?

After thousands of years of human history, Earth people recently gained the ability to fly and to communicate rapidly and broadly. Nearly everyone who lived prior to the past 100 years was subjected to only one conception of God because they never traveled more than 25 miles beyond their home, and rarely, if ever, met anyone who came from more than 25 miles away. Most people could not read and blindly accepted the "wisdom" of those who could.

So, of COURSE your concept of God should change, and continue to change. At least until you finish reading this book. Then it should stay rigid and unchanging for the rest of time.

148. CAN PEOPLE BE "BORN AGAIN?" DOES GOD DESIRE THIS?

What? Wasn't once enough?

149. WHAT DO YOU THINK OF
FUNDAMENTALISTS OF ANY RELIGION?

They are dangerous people who have no concept of how destructive they are. Even those who think of themselves as good people are doing harm to the Earth without realizing. God takes no sides for or against any people or any beliefs, but God finds that fundamentalists — those people who are most dogmatic and closed-minded, including some self-described atheists — are the least God-like.

People who are handed the supposed "truth," as in the Bible, and are content to accept it without questioning, are too dangerous to be trusted with it.

One of the worst things that many fundamentalists do is to poison the minds of children. They do so by putting a face on God. In most cases, it is a masculine face. Depicting an all-powerful being with masculine features teaches children that power is the domain of the male. It is a sexist lesson. It tends to omit and disenfranchise billions of people. Look around the Earth. Despite thousands of years of human history, women have yet to be treated as equals, even in the most enlightened societies. And in the least enlightened, women are scorned, degraded, enslaved, or even killed at birth. Most religions will not allow a woman to lead them. Why? If they believe that God created all beings, then don't they realize that God ensured that at least half the people on Earth are women? Do they believe that was some sort of aberration? God esteems women as much as men. There is no difference. Both are necessary for the continuation of the species. Women should not be put ON a pedestal or UNDER it. Yet that is exactly what happens when God is pictured as a man.

The solution is not, however, to begin depicting God as a woman or to try to ascribe any human attributes to

God. It would not be any improvement to have the pendulum swing the other way. Let God be God. Let people be people. THAT should be the fundamentals all people follow.

150. DIDN'T GOD KNOW IN ADVANCE ADAM AND EVE WOULD DISOBEY HIM?

In just 11 words, you have managed to make five huge – but common – mistakes. First, God does not know *any*thing in advance. Second, God is not a "him." Third, Adam and Eve did not even exist as depicted in the biblical story of creation. Fourth, God does not command humans to do anything. And fifth, people are not obliged to "obey" God.

I'm sorry. We don't mean to attack you. Your question is naïve, not really wrong, and you deserve an answer. But it is difficult for God to respond to a question that is based on an incorrect premise. We will try to rephrase the question for you. How about this: Did God try to direct the actions of the earliest humans, knowing they might not follow God's directions?

Well, this question is still not perfect. God, as you have learned elsewhere in this press conference, does not control or influence people in any way. Also, God has no psychic powers of prediction, although we do expect patterns of life on one planet to follow reasonably well the patterns of life on similar planets elsewhere in the cosmos. The story of Adam and Eve, however, is just plain wrong. Please read Question 212, What about "original sin?"

151. DID GOD ASK NOAH TO BUILD THE ARK?

No. Noah panicked. You must remember that Noah lived thousands of years ago, long before people had any understanding of weather patterns. It was a particularly rainy season, not unlike the monsoon rains that now drench Southeast Asia. Noah had a big family and much livestock. He was becoming concerned after a few days of rain as floodwaters began to rise. He had a small boat he had built, and decided that the land was no longer safe. Some of his animals had already drowned. He put his family on the boat, which didn't leave room for all his livestock, so he decided to take a male and a female of each type of animal with him, maybe a dozen animals in all. He pushed out from shore and soon was out in the sea far from land. He floated out there for what seemed like 40 days and 40 nights. At least, that's the story he told later.

In the middle of the sea, he could not see dry land, so he assumed it was all under water. Eventually, the tides carried him back to land. Noah thought his boat was standing still and the land was coming to *him*, pushing back the water as it came. Noah, you see, was a primitive farmer, and not very adept at scientific explanation, which in his day had not progressed very far. He saw many people and animals drowned, and the only explanation he could come up with was that God had punished them. What the story doesn't tell you is that he did find other people besides his family still alive. Otherwise, to whom would he tell his story? And like all sailors, he embellished it a little. So, suddenly he's got elephants and zebras and water buffalo on his boat. "Yeah, right," said all the other guys, and they rolled their eyes, and figured Noah had drunk a little too much salt water. But it made a good story, and it got repeated – and embellished – over the years until it turned into the story you know from the Bible.

Almost nothing about this story makes sense. We won't go into all the details here, but leave you with just one question: If the Bible story were true, what did the carnivores on the ark eat?

152. DID GOD WRITE THE 10 COMMANDMENTS?

No, God wrote the SEVEN commandments. But Moses was the original "Top 10 List" guy, so he added four and threw one away. He didn't think seven rules were impressive enough. "That's ALL?" he could imagine the Israelites saying. "God talks to you and all you bring back are seven rules?" (And why do I imagine that the Israelites sound exactly like Jackie Mason?) Plus, Moses wanted to make it look like God would be really ticked off if anyone questioned Moses' authority. Let's face it, Moses learned a lot about politics from Pharaoh, who was in some ways very much like a modern-day politician. The people Moses was leading from slavery in Egypt were not the best-educated bunch, and they tended to get a little rowdy, especially after that Red Sea fiasco (see the next question). So Moses decided to use a little good old-fashioned fear to keep them in line. He was sort of a one-man Department of Promised Land Security. Think of his Ten Commandments as a kind of Code Orange.

The original seven commandments were:
- Honor your father and mother
- Don't kill
- Don't commit adultery
- Don't steal
- Don't commit perjury
- Don't covet your neighbor's stuff
- Tip generously anyone who works for tips, but never more than 20%

Since Moses had no clue what God meant by the last one, he dropped this commandment, never realizing how much his descendants would need it.

God would never have bothered with the other four commandments about "no other gods" and keeping the Sabbath holy and "graven images." That was entirely Moses. Also, God is not so easily offended by people taking God's name in vain. (See Question 230 about blasphemy.)

153. ARE THERE ANGELS?

Yes, but they are not what you think. In fact, angels are not a "they." Angels are pure energy. Angels are the reason that the laws of physics work the same everywhere in all universes. Angels don't look at all like Roma Downey, Della Reese, or even Henry Travers (the angel Clarence in "It's a Wonderful Life"). When beings on another planet learned that Earth people have this image of goody-goody people with wings flying around and "fixing" things, they just about died laughing, and squirted krilbins out their zlurvs. Who comes up with this stuff? (See Question 129 about God's support staff.)

154. DID GOD BRING THE CHILDREN OF ISRAEL OUT OF EGYPT?

God assumes you are referring to what we call the "Red Sea Incident?" God had nothing to do with that. In fact, it did not happen at all the way it's described in the Torah. Water does not part like that. Face it, if you were an Israelite, would *you* want to walk between two huge walls of water? Think *you* would trust Moses that much?

It doesn't even make sense anyway. If God had parted the Red Sea, the sea bottom would not have been easy to walk on for even a few feet, much less a few miles. And what about all the sea life? Imagine what would have happened to all the sea life when those two walls came crashing back together. God would have to be mighty cruel to do that, even if God had taken sides against the Egyptians, which God would never have done.

That whole Moses history is such a crock. Sure there were plagues in Egypt. There were plagues everywhere in the world back then because modern medicine had not been discovered yet. The plagues did not come all together one after the other. They came years apart. But back then, people didn't want to tell stories that covered many years. So it got the Reader's Digest treatment. That means a lot of details got left out, such as that the Israelites fled across dry land, and the Egyptian soldiers were a day or two behind them. After they got a good ways out from Pharaoh's city, the soldiers just said, "Ah, the heck with it," and turned back, figuring the Israelites would die out there anyway. You can't judge these stories from a modern perspective. It's not like they had cell phones. Anyway, did you ever think about how this story even got reported? It sure as Saturn's rings wasn't the Egyptians who wrote it down the way you've read it. And just how would the Israelites know what happened to the Egyptian soldiers? Like most Bible stories, this one doesn't bear much scrutiny, but it makes a nice campfire story. Over the centuries of retelling before it was written down, it just got more and more adventuresome.

155. IS THERE SUCH A THING AS THE HOLY GRAIL? IF SO, WHAT IS IT AND WHERE IS IT?

There is not just one Holy Grail, and none of them are real, physical things. They are the desires of humankind to see beyond itself. Hardly anyone, not even your self-described atheists, wants this life – whatever it is – to be IT. Some people want to experience another life after this one. Other people are content to know that there is *something* out there beyond their senses that exists and will exist after they are gone. Each of these desires is a Holy Grail, which sometimes gets represented by a symbol, such as a chalice. The most common symbol, of course, is the cup used by Jesus Christ at his last meal before execution. Was there such a cup? Of course there was. He had to have taken a drink from something, right? If this cup still existed, and if it could be identified beyond any doubt as Christ's final cup, and if anyone ever found this cup and recognized it... they would immediately set themselves a new quest, a new Grail. It is not in your nature ever to stop questioning the infinite. A very fine troupe of actors on the planet PwiQtlspa[3], who look very much like you Earthlings, has managed to completely stop asking such questions, but it's doubtful that you ever will. Even after you read this book.

---

[3] Pronounced pee-week&etul-spa, where the & means to swallow quickly and no syllable is emphasized

156. ARE THERE MIRACLES?

Do you mean, does God perform miracles? No, God does not intervene in mundane affairs. The unexpected and often wonderful things that happen, those things people call "miracles," are just the upside of chaos. There's a downside to chaos as well, of course.

Take the recent case of young Elizabeth Smart, kidnapped from her home in the middle of the night by a raving lunatic, then discovered alive and returned to her family eight months later. Her father happily declared it a miracle, and no doubt, to him it seemed to be one. Yet he did not consider the full import of his words. If God were going to get involved in saving this young girl, why not get involved much earlier and keep her from being taken in the first place? So, when people thank God for resolving some horrible situation, they are also implying that God was sleeping on the job when the situation turned horrible in the first place. The bad things and the good things in life happen without any help from God. (See Question 77, Why do bad things happen to good people?) Having said that, don't rule out the possible intervention of some force other than God. Intelligent beings from other planets have been known to dabble in Earth matters from time to time.

When the Catholic Church officially proclaims something a "miracle," we always pay attention, 'cause these guys have _standards_, standards for measuring what is and what is not a miracle. According to *The Catholic Encyclopedia*, "the miracle is called supernatural, because the effect is beyond the productive power of nature and implies supernatural agency." There's a whole raft of ways to measure an event against this standard. The problem with the arguments of people who set out to prove that there ARE miracles is that they almost all go back to some source such as the Bible, which is about as reliable a proof of miracles as "Aesop's Fables."

You want miracles? Hold up your hand and look at it carefully. There are 27 bones in there, packaged in a most delicate way, and with an opposable thumb that gives humans special abilities, almost unique among all animals. The complexities of your hand are symbolic of the complexities of *all* life. The magnitude of those complexities – of hands, of brains, of your very capacity to recreate yourself, to be born and to give birth – is what leads many people to proclaim the miracles of God. They see miracles everywhere, and they say, "Can you not see that only a God could create life, could perform such miracles?" Yet the greater miracle is what actually occurred, which is that evolution continually improves on God's original creations. God is not some Frank Lloyd Wright sitting around designing arteries and muscles and bones and skin. In fact, if God were to design people, then you humans would be a lot better built than you are. It's kind of insulting to say that Earth people are the best God could do, with your flimsy bodies and susceptibility to disease and puny brains. If God WERE designing people, you'd look a lot different. If God had the power suggested in the Bible and other myths, then creating something like people could hardly be considered miraculous. The real miracle is that your hand, that incredible instrument, evolved *without* God's intervention.

157. WE'VE READ ABOUT SOME OF THE ANCIENT
EVENTS AND ATTITUDES THAT MADE GOD
ANGRY. ARE THERE NEW TOPICS OR TYPES OF
THINGS THAT WEREN'T AROUND WHEN THE
HOLY BOOKS WERE BEING WRITTEN THAT WE
SHOULD WATCH OUT FOR?

Well, God – not being a mind reader – is not sure what kinds of things you have in mind. We suppose you might mean the way awesome weapons like firearms and missiles change the power equation among tribes, or the culture collisions that were impossible before high-speed travel and telecommunications. These things are of no consequence to God.

There's a major fallacy in your question. Just because a book tells you that there are events and behaviors that make God angry, does not make it so. As we said earlier, God does not feel emotions. Don't think of God as just another person, but bigger and cooler. It is impossible to upset or anger God. Books like the Bible are a poor record of history and an even worse observation of God. God did not write the Bible, the Torah, or the Koran. God did not cause them to be written. God is not even a contributing editor or guest commentator. For the most part, God comes off as a nasty, humorless, backstabbing, jealous hypocrite in these books, displaying all the behaviors that God supposedly told people NOT to exhibit. Why does anyone think God would deliberately create such an unflattering self-portrait?

158. WHAT DOES GOD THINK OF THE CRUSADES AND OTHER RELIGIOUS WARS?

First, let me put to rest the idea that God "thinks." God is a doer, not a thinker. God does not ponder God's next actions like some chess master, and God does not contemplate the human condition. If God *did* think about the many ways and reasons that you Earth people have found to destroy and torture each other, and allowed it to continue, what would that say about God's concern for your well-being? How can anyone see what happens on Earth and still think of God as a kind of proud parent or good shepherd?

Sadly, there are people who take God's lack of intervention to mean that God approves of the horrible things they do. And so, people kill in the name of religion. And they claim power in the name of God. And they tell women that they must cover their heads or submit to their husbands. And they kill and suppress Blacks and Jews and Catholics and Buddhists and atheists and Shiites and gays and anyone who doesn't *think* right or *look* right. And they act righteous with no more authority to do so than their own imagination. And God does nothing about it, because God is NOT the God they have fantasized.

So, the great villains of history have convinced themselves that God must be on their side. Yet they conveniently overlook the obvious evidence that they are no more favored by God than is the air they breathe. What is this evidence? That there are so *many* religious wars and crusades that succeed in destroying billions of people and converting the survivors to think like their conquerors, and that it is impossible for every one of these fanatics to have the one true religion. Muslims kill the infidels and claim that God gave them victory. And then Christians kill the Muslims and claim that God gave *them* the victory. And Catholics hate Protestants while Protestants hate Catholics and Shiites hate Sunnis and Hindus hate Muslims and everyone hates the Jews who claim that *they* are God's chosen people, and where is the logic in *ANY* of it? God disavows ALL religion and all who fight with swords OR WITH WORDS in God's name.

159. DO WE NEED TO BE SAVED? IF SO, FROM WHAT?

A better question might be saved FOR what? You people are not like some sort of living currency that God wants to save for a rainy day. When you die, you vanish, permanently. Your body returns to the natural world. Your soul and your thoughts cease. No part of you "goes to God." No, you don't need to be saved in any lasting sense. But you do need to be better shepherds of your environment so that your species may continue for the billions of years that Earth will continue to exist.

160. DOES GOD LISTEN TO PRAYERS?

Praying allows a person who may be otherwise helpless to feel that he or she is doing *something* to improve a situation. It is generally motivated by good intentions, and it often helps the person praying to feel better. The only problem is that God is not listening.

People who put themselves "in God's hands" and refuse medical care and immunizations are, essentially, gamblers, which is ironic, since most of them forbid gambling. Some of them WILL get better, but God was not blowing on their dice, so to speak.

Prayer is the ultimate act of arrogance, especially any prayer that is not motivated by desperate measures. It's understandable that someone who is desperate – afraid for their own health and well-being or that of a dear one – would hope for intervention by anyone or anything. Cynical people like to say, "There are no atheists in foxholes." That's utter Taurus quasars of course, for someone who is truly atheistic does not suddenly change his or her entire belief system when scared. Just because one hopes for *something* to keep them safe from harm does not mean they truly believe that a God will listen or intervene.

But non-desperate prayer is pure arrogance. It assumes that what the pray-er wants is not in conflict with what someone else wants. For example, some people rejoice that their prayer for a sunny day was answered, though someone else prayed just as fervently that it would rain. Does this mean that the "loser" is less favored by God than the "winner?" To assume that God takes sides at all, and that in particular, if you are good enough, God will take *your* side is nothing but arrogance. It's the Santa Claus myth run amok, as if God were making a list, and checking it twice, to decide which person's wish to grant.

By the way... Did you ever notice that in the version of God that many of you Earthlings believe, God comes off an awful lot like Santa Claus? At first, little Christians get wonderful surprise gifts delivered by an invisible, benevolent old bearded guy who sees them when they're sleeping and knows if they are bad or good. Then, they learn the truth, but – and here's the good part – they still get gifts! They don't need to believe in Santa to get the things they want. They just need to "be good."

Sports competition is the perfect example of arrogant prayer. A batter who prays as he steps to the plate is asking God to favor him at the expense of the pitcher and the other team, and *they're* probably praying just as hard for the batter to strike out, or, if it's a Little League game, they may be praying just as hard that if the batter hits it, the ball goes somewhere else.

Prayer that asks no intercession but only seeks to praise and thank God is no better, for this prayer assumes that people are so important that God would be insulted if not thanked. Imagine that you are the sales manager at a mid-size company. You just negotiated a sales contract that will help your company and create good jobs for several people. Do you now expect those people you've helped to *praise* you? No. Only a real loser demands praise for doing well what they do normally. So, if you feel that God deserves and needs praise, then aren't you really saying that God is an egotistical and insufferable fool? At the same time, aren't you exaggerating your own importance to God?

Finally, consider the person who believes that God is not a thinking Supreme Being, but is just a force that created everything in the universe, including the laws of physics. Is it not even more arrogant for this person to pray? After all, they are not offering their words of hope to a listening being, but just assuming that somehow the universe will accommodate itself to their individual needs.

Prayer is surrender. Prayer is the opposite of taking responsibility for one's own actions. Prayer is expecting – or at least hoping – to be helped just because one asks, not because one is necessarily deserving or has done anything to help themselves. The wisest advice has always been "God helps those who help themselves." Following that advice, one should resist the temptation to pray.

Wow! I see that answer sure got your hands flying. I have to give that last questioner a chance to follow up. Go ahead.

161. Thank you. YOU HAVEN'T SAID WHETHER GOD IS INFLUENCED BY PRAYER, OR DID GOD SET EVERYTHING IN MOTION AND SIT BACK AND LET IT HAPPEN THROUGH NATURAL LAW?

Some choice! No, God is not influenced by prayer. Although the act of praying can be helpful, the same way taking a placebo can be helpful, God has never intervened in the course of a life in response to prayer. Of course, some prayers appear to be answered. Believers can give you hundreds or thousands of examples when the thing for which someone prayed came true. They conveniently overlook or explain away the millions of examples of prayers every day that have no impact, much the way your friend who went to the casino last year only told you about what he won, and wants to forget about how much he lost.

Cardinal Joseph Ratzinger was elected in 2005 to be the new Pope, and took the name Pope Benedict XVI. After his election, he said that he prayed fervently *not* to be elected, but that God chose not to honor his wishes. Perhaps it would have helped if Ratzinger had told some of his fellow cardinals that he did not want to serve. Was God supposed to fill out their ballots for them or whisper in their ears, "Pssst. Don't vote for Ratzinger"?

On the other hand, God is not "sitting back," either. Don't think of God as some blasé CEO who is watching each person on a hidden TV camera, deciding when to take action and when to back off. Everything that happens, happens on its own. Is that what you mean by "natural law?"

162. CAN PRAYER HELP THE PERSON WHO IS PRAYING OR OTHER PEOPLE NOT EVEN IN THE ROOM?

A person who prays for healing, for example, may, indeed, see healing occur, but that has nothing to do with God. It is the power of positive thinking.

As for remote "intercessory" prayer, God would now be rolling on the floor with laughter, if God laughed, or could roll, or there were a floor.

Forget those studies that show it works. They're bunk, and they insult God (who, by the way, cannot feel insulted or any other emotion). God is not so cruel as to help only those people for whom a stranger prays. In fact, this whole idea defies logic.

Suppose a devout person in Springfield learns there is a very sick person in the next state, and begins to pray. Heck, say that 100 people in Springfield get together to pray for this stranger we'll call Hasenpfeffer. They don't tell anyone else what they're doing, not even Hasenpfeffer. There's a patient in the bed next to Hasenpfeffer, just as sick, but Springfield doesn't pray for that person we'll call Ambrosia. These Springfielders actually *expect* Hasenpfeffer to get better while Ambrosia stays sick or gets worse. And they think that God would be a party to this vicious lottery. They treat God like some Emergency Hotline phone operator, just waiting around for a "call" before going off to help heal someone. Give us a break!

These are the same people who think God sees everything and can control everything. (If you don't think God can fix it, why bother asking?) Yet somehow, they think, God just missed knowing about Ambrosia and Hasenpfeffer, and won't spring into action until enough prayers have come in, like Batman waiting for the Bat

Signal. "Well, gee, no one's praying for Ambrosia. Guess I can't help *that* poor sucker out." Even if God *did* intercede, do these people think that God would base a decision like that only on who receives prayer support? There would be lots of other factors to consider. Maybe Hasenpfeffer *wants* to die. Maybe Ambrosia is a nicer person, or is about to have a child, or is a lot younger. Intercessory prayer ignores all those factors.

But if you ever needed proof that God does not intervene based on prayer, look no farther than your tragic day of September 11, 2001. On that day, 19 devout Muslims hijacked four jets, intent on crashing them into crowded public buildings. The hijackers and their co-conspirators prayed fervently before and during the hijackings for Allah[4] to make them successful. On board Flight 93, passengers learned that planes had been deliberately flown into the World Trade Center, and they prayed for God to help them prevent their plane from a similar fate. Through cell phones, they told people on the ground, "Pray for us," as they charged their captors. Flight 93 crash-landed in rural Pennsylvania, killing dozens, but probably saving hundreds of lives by not reaching its hijackers' destination. Americans rightly praised the passengers' courage, and some people said that the prayers were answered.

If that's the case, if you can infer from the "success" of Flight 93's passengers, that God played a role in what happened, then isn't it just as likely that God played a role in the fate of the other three jets? Or do you think God ignored the prayers of the passengers on the doomed jets, or was only going to save one jet anyway? What the heck kind of view of God is that? Why would God want to grant

---

[4] Remember: "Allah" is just another name for "God." We're talking about the same deity here.

163

the prayers of the hijackers for a while, and *then* capriciously turn around and grant the prayers of the innocents they wanted to kill? Neither the Muslims nor the Christians nor anyone else should feel that God was on their side or answered *anyone's* prayer.

163. DO FAITH HEALERS ACTUALLY WORK?

Oh, puh-leeze! God does not respond to even the most sincere entreaties for help, much less the self-serving shows put on by quacks who are just ripping off nice but gullible people.

Having said that, some people *will* get better because they have a good attitude about their condition. In that sense, their faith may benefit them, with or without the help of a con artist. God does not smite people, but if God were ever tempted to do so, faith healers would be among the first to get zapped.

164. THERE HAVE BEEN MANY PROPHETS THROUGHOUT TIME; HOW DOES ONE DIFFERENTIATE BETWEEN THE MINOR PROPHETS AND THOSE WHO WERE FOUNDERS OF INDEPENDENT FAITHS?

I see this question as a deeper concern about the very existence of prophets. For if God DID send prophets to Earth or sent messages directly to people who then *became* prophets, why would God designate some as minor and give others the task of founding complete religions? (See Question 145, Have you sent prophets to Earth?)

For that matter, why would God WANT different complete religions? If nothing else convinces you that God does not take sides, it should be that. We don't understand why you Earth people are convinced that God prefers some of you to others of you. People have set up two possible views of God. Earthlings who believe that God created only one religion, and that they happen to belong to that "One True Religion," dismiss people of any other belief system or culture. They believe, in other words, that the God they love so much would just toy with everyone else, create them for nothing more than amusement. Or the other possibility is that God *did* create competing religions, which really doesn't say a lot of nice things about God, does it?

Let's say that God set up different prophets through the ages. Many of these prophets, or the people we call prophets, are reporting very similar messages from God to people. But a lot of them don't agree with each other. And there have been many *additional* self-proclaimed prophets whose messages died with them and were not recorded for posterity. That raises just four possibilities about all these known and unknown prophets:

1) They were all prophets, but they were given different and sometimes contradictory messages;

165

2) They were all prophets, but the messages from God changed over time (sometimes just weeks or months apart);

3) Some were true prophets and some were not, which explains why some "got it wrong;" or

4) None of them were true prophets, there is no such thing as a true prophet, and none of the messages they "brought" were authentic.

That's it! There are no other possible explanations for whether there are or are not prophets. So, why do people who believe in prophets pick just a few to follow? If God has prophets among Earth people, on what basis does someone decide which reported prophets to believe, while deciding that others who claimed to be prophets were phonies? Or do they think that God keeps sending more messengers, because God wants to update the data God is sharing with people? Kind of like a football coach sending in a new play at the last second. Basically, people who follow just a few so-called prophets see God as either indecisive or amazingly flexible, OR they think that there are one heck of a lot of phony prophets. And it is only in this final regard that they are correct.

God does not call the plays here on Earth. You people do that yourselves. Sometimes among you there are people with some pretty good ideas for how to live life better, but there is no one-size-fits-all religion. How could there be? Look at how different people are! So, you get different "teachers," different "advisers" among you, and you call some of them "prophets." They are no different than you. God speaks no more to them than to you. Their minds and their hearts simply work in different ways than yours, and people choose to listen to them for one reason or another.

So, to answer the question, no. There are no minor prophets. There are only minor people.

165. I have to follow up. IF ALL RELIGIONS "HAVE IT WRONG," WHAT DO YOU THINK OF THE MINISTERS, RABBIS, PRIESTS, MULLAHS, AND OTHERS WHO SPEAK FOR THESE RELIGIONS?

Most of them are good, well-meaning, honest people who don't have a prayer (pardon the pun) of getting to the truth or sharing it with others because, in almost all cases, they are starting from a flawed perspective.

It's as if L. Frank Baum had claimed that "The Wizard of Oz" was revealed truth, told to him directly by God. Today, people would be arguing over the real message of the tin man and the scarecrow, and building altars to Dorothy and Toto. By accepting as historical fact the fables and myths of the Bible and other religious texts, religious teachers are doomed before they begin.

When these religious teachers share ideas and perspectives without insisting that theirs is the only correct "truth," they help advance humanity to new levels of development. When they act to close minds to new ideas, they destroy humanity and act against God. There's never been a good idea in all of human history that couldn't be bludgeoned to death by a few zealots or folks of low intellect or education. Take socialism, or even communism. Take the Taliban or Khmer Rouge. Take pretty much *all* your fundamentalists... *please.* These and other ideology-based movements or regimes all had at least a kernel of a good idea, and demolished it.

166. WHAT DOES GOD THINK OF RELIGIOUS SCHOOLS?

God has no problem with religious schools of any religion that teach respect for ALL of God's creations, including people of another religion. There is nothing inherently wrong with parents wanting their children to learn and understand the *parents'* beliefs and moral codes, except if that moral code includes the mistreatment or annihilation of other people or of the environment. God does not want schools to teach children to worship God, but rather to respect God's creations. If a parent wants their child in a religious school that emphasizes one particular religion, God wants you to know that's just fine.

But if a child is in a school with other children who may not share that same religious belief, no matter how admirable it may be, then God would hope that all beliefs – some of which may not be spoken for fear of negative consequences – would be equally respected. No one should be forced to listen to someone else's smoky idea of religion. That should be especially true in schools, where the susceptible minds of children should not be involuntarily subjected to prayers or sermons espousing any point of view, including atheism. One-size-fits-all religion, or lack of religion, has never succeeded in making any country or planet stronger.

167. WE'VE BEEN THINKING ABOUT WHO
SHOULD BE AUTHORIZED TO STUDY AND
SPREAD YOUR WORD. DOES GOD HAVE TROUBLE
WITH WOMEN, GAY PEOPLE, OR YOUNGSTERS
BEING PRIESTS?

Well, since God does not prefer any person or type of person over any other, why would God have trouble with anything God created? God does not make the rules for people, and that's something worth celebrating. YOU make your own rules, and don't have to worry about God playing Almighty Supreme Court Chief Justice on you. If you don't want gay people or women preaching to you, that is your prerogative, but don't try to justify your bigotry by saying that _God_ told you to be intolerant, or by thinking you know what God wants.

God does not have any word that needs to be spread. God never sent any prophets to Earth to speak for God. God does not speak to Earthlings or to any other beings in anything you would call "language." God needs no words, so God does not care what words people choose. Priests and ministers and rabbis and teachers and philosophers are jobs YOU choose, not jobs that God assigns. These people are not "authorized" to speak for God.

God is not the Great Personnel Director in the sky. God does not study each person and decide what they will be or assign them a job. That's SO Communist China.

168. MANY PEOPLE ASK GOD, "WHY?" BUT I'D
LIKE TO ASK, "WHY NOT?"

The answer to both questions would be the same, and the reason both why and why not is: Change. Evolution. The only reason that something does not exist or happen is because change decreed it would not. Some call that "Fate." God says, "Anti-matter happens."

169. OH LORD, GOD OF HEAVEN AND EARTH, WE WORSHIP AND PRAISE YOUR GRACE. PLEASE SHOW US YOUR WILL IN OUR LIVES AND IN A WAY THAT WE CAN UNDERSTAND. PLEASE WATCH OVER AND PROTECT OUR CHILDREN AND HELP US TO TEACH THEM IN YOUR LOVE. YOUR GOODNESS AND GRACE ARE BEYOND OUR COMPREHENSION; PLEASE GRANT US A GLIMPSE OF YOUR GREATNESS SO THAT OUR FAITH MAY BE STRONG. *

What, again?! How much more of a "glimpse' do you need? (See Question 41, Why are you invisible?) Just take a look at the pictures from the Hubble telescope if you want a glimpse of what God has created.

This kind of "prayer" is exactly what God is talking about throughout this book. It's pushy and demanding and arrogant. It treats God as if God were Marlon Brando in "The Godfather." (Even that name – "Godfather" – shows how much people have grown to think of those two very different terms together: God and Father. "Our Father who art in heaven," and "Our heavenly Father," and on and on *ad nauseum.* No wonder people get the wrong idea about God.)

On the one hand, this prayer is cloying and subservient, essentially kowtowing before God and kissing God's metaphorical ring. "We praise your grace." That might seem a lot more sincere if it were not followed by an immediate expression of doubt about that very "grace." This person wants it all spelled out nice and neat and easy, in a way they can "understand." Unfortunately, life is not that easy, and God is not Don Corleone.

VII. WAR AND OTHER NASTY BEHAVIOR
Or, ALL WE ARE SAYING IS GIVE PEAS A CHANCE

Probably the first bit of logic that each of us learned is that if A equals B, then B must also equal A. Then we hear that "war is hell," and we make the logical assumption that hell must also be war, a place of constant turmoil and struggle and pain.

No behavior on Earth causes more grief and pain than war. The evil that spawns war and the evil that occurs in war are both frightening and fascinating. No behavior is more examined. You fight wars and then you write books about them for centuries afterwards. You make dozens, if not hundreds, of movies about each war. You build statues to your warriors and monuments to honor your dead. You rarely go more than a few years without fighting a war, and yet insist that you hate war above all else. No wonder we got so many questions about war and killing and evil.

170. HOW DO YOU EXPLAIN WAR?

There are so many flaws in human beings. You do not share easily. Right? That came hard. You are territorial. You harbor jealousies. You are never glad when someone else gets something good that you did not get more of. *You* see these flaws in your daily lives, at school, at work. You cannot understand how each other person can be so petty, right?

Wars like World War II are bound to happen. All the small problems, the small flaws, became concentrated in time like rays of light focused through a magnifying glass to ignite a fire. Every bad impulse of humanity is unleashed at once. But like every immense fire, most wars burn out rather quickly. Humanity will never free itself of its flaws or its wars.

The best you can do about wars is to keep alive the desire to avoid them and, when they occur, do what you can to control them and end them. God notes that Earthlings, alone among all the species in the universe, have developed the means and the will to destroy themselves. Every other species fights against extinction, fights against those actions that will wipe itself out. But not humankind.

You work hard to educate yourselves to make more powerful weapons every generation. For thousands of years, you Earthlings have sought better, more efficient ways to kill other Earthlings. First, a man picked up a rock and bludgeoned another man with it. Then he discovered he could get the same result without putting himself in harm's way if he THREW the rock from a safe distance. He then figured out to sharpen certain rocks before throwing, and then how to project a sharp rock with greater force by making a slingshot, and then an arrow. And every generation learned how to aim it more accurately, to be more deadly. And finally, man figured out how to simulate a million sharp rocks firing all at once in many directions. Bombs. And bigger bombs to scare the little bomb throwers. (By the way, did you notice that all these "advances" were thought of and developed by men, not women? Shouldn't that tell you something?)

Each generation says it must protect itself from the horrible new rock that inevitably falls into the hands of some destructive person. It is human nature to seek protection, to fear the destroyer. Yet it is also human nature to learn how to destroy.

171. HOW DOES A GOOD GOD ACCOUNT FOR EVIL IN THE WORLD?

The fallacy in your question is the assumption that God is good. (See Question 17, Are you all good?) God is just God, neither good nor bad.

Another problem with this question is the definition of "evil." We suspect you mean those things done by some humans that have a negative impact on the environment or quality of life of other humans. The word "evil" implies intent. If something bad happens that no one intended to happen, most of you – except, of course, for certain lawyers – accept it and move on. Therefore, you usually do not say that the destructive acts of nature or of other animals are evil. A volcano, for example, is not evil. A hawk feeding on a helpless rodent is not evil.

The things you consider evil are of no interest to God. God did not make them evil, and has no ability to predict when evil will occur or to make something stop being evil. God does not intervene at all, and cannot begin to explain why one person becomes evil and another does not.

Neither evil nor its solution comes from God. As we've said before, the bad news is, you're on your own. The GOOD news is, you're on your own. (See Question 232 about children who suffer and Question 179 about the justification for war.)

172. IS KILLING ANOTHER PERSON EVER JUSTIFIED?

Surprisingly, yes! God deplores the destruction of the things and life forms that God created. No one should ever kill another person, period! But if you are sure, beyond a shadow of a doubt, that one person is just about to kill another, no matter what the reason, then you must prevent that murder. If the only way to prevent it is to kill the person, you are justified to do so.

The problem is figuring out who decides that killing is justified. Remember, you can prevent murder by taking away the would-be murderer's means of killing (his or her guns, bombs, etc.) or opportunity to kill (by, for example, locking him or her away). You cannot kill someone if you just *suspect* they may be contemplating murder. (And, by the way, NEVER rely on psychics to tell you what someone will do in the future. Even God cannot predict the future, so no mere human will ever have that power.)

173. WHAT ABOUT KILLING ONESELF? HOW DOES GOD FEEL ABOUT SUICIDE?

God does not "feel" about anything. What would you even *want* God to feel? Regret? Anger? Shame? But if God did "feel" about suicide, God would remind you that there are no acts that are absolutely wrong 100 percent of the time. (See Question 210, Are there moral absolutes?) Suicide can be a cowardly act or a brave one. It can hurt the dead person's family and friends terribly, or it can give them great relief in spite of any sadness they feel. Suicide is the destruction of a precious creation, but it can be so much more than that. Remember that a life that ends is not necessarily a life "cut short." (See Question 112, Why do people die seemingly before their time?)

175

174. IS IT MORALLY DEFENSIBLE TO KILL BUGS? AS I WAS GARDENING, THERE WERE ANTS AND SPIDERS AND SOME OTHER CREEPY-CRAWLIES... I KILLED THEM ALL – NO ONE WAS SPARED. NOW, I KNOW ANTS DON'T HURT ME, AND WHILE SPIDERS SCARE THE BEJEZUS OUT OF ME, I KNOW THEY ARE SUPPOSED TO BE GOOD FOR THE GARDEN. BUT FRANKLY, I JUST DON'T CARE. I SQUASH THEM ALL. I WOULDN'T KILL A CAT OR DOG OR EVEN A SQUIRREL, AND WOULD LET MICE BE (AS LONG AS THEY ARE OUTSIDE!). BUT WHAT IS IT ABOUT BUGS? THEIR SIZE? THEIR APPEARANCE? AM I A BUG HITLER?

You might be. You have probably noticed that it does not work to be nice to bugs. They are extraordinarily ignorant. They wish to devour you, infect your food, or climb in orifices of your body where they don't belong. There is no reason for you to like or condone this behavior.

Therefore, it's okay to kill bugs when and if they invade your space and cause sickness or distress. Don't go killing them when they are in THEIR space, such as a park, a marsh, a dog's fur (unless the dog is yours). If they will keep to their environment and stay out of yours, you can have a detente. Try to stay out of THEIR way, and they need to stay out of YOURS. If you have wandered into their home area and they defend themselves, that's fair, and you should back off. Expect the same in return. If they insist on being in your house or on (or in) your body, they are going to get killed, and that seems only fair.

We see no moral conflict here. You are only a Hitler to the bugs if you condemn as many as possible to die no matter what they have done to you. If you go out of your way to find them and annihilate them, you are a big meanie, and someday the Chief Bug will get you for that.

176

175. WHOSE SIDE IS GOD ON IN WAR? HOW DOES GOD DECIDE WHOM TO SUPPORT?

God does not take sides. War is all about destruction. We are appalled at how many people destroy God's creations in the *name* of God. From our perspective there is only animal, vegetable, mineral, and energy. Nothing about sides. One animal eats another. Whose side should God be on? The carnivore lives only because the other animal dies. Should the carnivore die? You know, plants die when they get eaten, too. Don't plants get a side?

Now, if you mean, which people does God like, that's different. God does not have a "chosen people," although God rather favors a particular group of beings on another planet. Part of the problem is that too many Earthlings pray too much. We don't mind the conversation, but sometimes it gets a little pushy. Athletes. Athletes who pray for help are the worst! What do they need God's help for? Can't they do this on their own? Wouldn't it <u>mean</u> more if they do it without God guiding the ball or the bat? And anyway, when one athlete thrives, it usually means another one fails, so we don't take sides. Although it would be nice if the Cubs could win a World Series. (See Questions 160-162 about prayer.)

176. DO YOU HAVE ANY THOUGHTS ON HOW TO STOP ALL OF THOSE IDIOTS WHO CLAIM TO BE DOING GOD'S WILL? THE MOST OBVIOUS EXAMPLE, OF COURSE, IS THAT OF WAGING WAR AND KILLING PEOPLE IN GOD'S NAME.

Did you ever notice that those "idiots" all die, the same as everyone else? That usually stops them. If you want to stop them sooner, you'll have to come up with something on your own.

177. WHY DO HUMANS FIGHT WITH EACH OTHER SO MUCH? WHAT IS *THAT* ABOUT?

That's about competition, which seems to be rife in your DNA. Almost everything is a "sport" to you Earthlings. You even count the bodies in a disaster! Why? Is it important to someone who lost a loved one to know exactly how many other people are suffering, too? It's meaningless. But it gives you the chance to compare disasters, like a sporting event. "My calamity is bigger than YOUR calamity." You talk about which caused more financial damage, which killed more people, which destroyed more homes, etc. You measure *everything*: earthquake intensity and wind speed and the size of just about anything. Size is always important to you. And you keep these records FOREVER, like it mattered.

It's also about being right, another annoying trait of humans. If your candidate "wins," somehow it justifies your beliefs, even if 49.9 percent of the vote went for the other person. You can conveniently forget that they exist, and hope that the winner ignores their beliefs or desires.

This compulsion to be "right" manifests itself most strongly – and most dangerously – in religion. "My God is mightier than YOUR God," seems to be the credo, as if there were competing gods instead of just one. Perhaps the confusion stems from the fact that each language gives God a different name (see Question 127), leading to the notion that these are different gods. We've seen Christians holding signs that read "Allah sucks" or similar elegant terms. Would they hold up a sign that says, "God sucks?" That is, after all, what their sign means. And, of course, many Muslims fail to grasp that the Allah that created them is the same one that created every Jew and Christian and Buddhist and pagan.

So, you fight over almost everything: to prove your idea of a merciful God is more correct than someone else's idea; to prove that you have bigger guns; to prove that *your* men are more manly than *their* men. And you fight over resources. You are willing to kill to take what you want, whether it is oil or water or food. The more desperately you need those things, the more violent you become to obtain them. Yet despite your pathetic nature as a species, you insist you are made in God's image. As if.

178. SO MUCH VIOLENCE AND KILLING ARE DONE IN GOD'S NAME. WHY DOESN'T GOD STEP FORWARD AND DECLARE AN END TO THIS MADNESS BEFORE WE ARE ALL ANNIHILATED?

What makes you think that God has not already "stepped" forward? Your question implies that God is somehow absent, that God has abandoned you Earth people. In a sense, of course, you are correct, because God is not involved in your squabbles and wars. God is not some father figure directly out of Central Casting, just waiting for the right moment to enter the room and separate the fighting siblings.

The ancient Greek playwrights had a term for it — *deus ex machina*, God from the machine. Whenever a playwright painted his characters into a corner, *ZAP!...* God suddenly and magically solved everything. Playwrights and screenwriters today still employ this device. Real life, unfortunately, does not come with devices. God will not be appearing in your local war zone and, like James Bond, cutting just the right wire at the last instant to prevent annihilation. You're going to need to get yourself out of this jam. God suggests you don't wait too long to get started.

179. WHAT ARE GOD'S THOUGHTS ABOUT WAR? IS IT EVER JUSTIFIED? WILL WAR EVER END?

That's a good question. The simple answer is that there always seems to be an excuse to start a *new* one. No one ever started a war because things were going so well that they just had to kill someone to celebrate. War is *always* the result of a failure of some kind, and of betrayal.

War is as old as humanity on Earth, and its legacy may be the end of people on Earth unless the pattern of war is changed, which will take great will and great strength. Consider this pattern. The very first battle between humans occurs when one primitive man throws a rock at another in anger. The second man throws a bigger rock. Next comes a sharper rock, and then a sharper rock attached to a stick to extend the warrior's reach. Then the stick becomes a spear with a sharp rock on its end, capable of being thrown so that the warrior can be farther away from his target. Next comes the bow, capable of launching the spear with greater force and from a greater distance. Somewhere along the way, a person picks up a thin, flat rock and uses it as a shield. Another person discovers that metal hammered into a disc makes an even better shield.

And so, the development of weaponry takes on a life of its own. Each generation of weapons is more destructive than the last. One tribe invents a more powerful weapon, so the other tribe copies it or builds an equal defense, believing that parity equals security. Each time one tribe learns new ways to kill, the other side catches up. Humanity's quest for supremacy leads to gunpowder, and bullets, and bombs, and nuclear missiles. Each new weapon is designed to undo the balance of power, to give its bearer the offensive edge. Earth people have reached, in an incredibly short time – a time too short for people to realize fully what they have done – the point where additional or more powerful weapons are superfluous, because today's weapons are now capable of complete annihilation in a matter of minutes, making such annihilation extremely likely. Earth people have virtually perfected the science of killing. Now the question is whether you will similarly perfect the art of peace.

How do wars start? They start because of bad choices. Let's say that you know someone hates you. For now, don't worry whether they are justified in hating you or not. They hate you, period. What can you do about it? Basically, you have four options:

1) Let them go on hating you, and accept the consequences of that hatred, which may mean that some of your citizens get hurt or killed or suffer some other form of punishment. Accept these consequences as stoically as possible.

2) Let them go on hating you, and react only if they begin to inflict some punishment on you or your citizens, at which point you can take appropriate countermeasures to make them stop this punishment.

3) Don't wait for them to act. The best defense is to bully them, insult them, punish them, and even kill them before they can get to you.

4) Figure out why they hate you, and see what you can do to reduce that hatred before either their citizens or yours get hurt.

There are no other options that are not some form of one of these four. Which option do you think God would choose? No matter which side you are on, no matter whether you've done something "wrong" or not, there is *never* a justification for war. *Always* choose number four.

180. Please permit me to follow up, Jeremiah. IS THERE
SUCH A THING AS A GOOD WAR?
Never. But sometimes there is such a thing as an
unavoidable war. Note God did not say "necessary." War is
never necessary, but defending oneself may be impossible to
avoid.

The worst thing is starting a war, even if you are
convinced that you will soon be attacked. If no one ever starts a
war, there will never be a war. It's that simple. Preventing war
is rather like trying to prevent crime. You cannot arrest a
person because they are likely to commit a crime, but you can
remove their opportunity to do so, and you can convince them
that if they do commit the crime, they will be severely punished.
After that, all you can do is hope they are responsible and
responsive to their fear of punishment. If they don't commit the
crime, you've done well to deter them. If they do, you are there
to make sure they never do it again.

And so, among nations, you must be vigilant, but you
must never "punish" the "crime" not yet committed by firing the
first shot.

Consider the driver of a car who kills or injures someone
in an accident and then claims they were "under the influence" of
drugs or alcohol. You don't accept that as an excuse, and you
shouldn't. Yet when someone claims they are "under the
influence" of God, you *do* accept it as a reasonable, if not entirely
rational, excuse. Isn't it really the *same* excuse? Aren't both
people claiming that some external force impaired or guided
their judgment? At least, with the first person, the claim is true.
Drugs and alcohol DO impair judgment, but God does not. God
has NEVER directed anyone to kill or to behave a certain way.
Wars and violence committed in the name of God are a sham,
and God denounces them!

183

181. My question is a follow-up to what that last person asked. ARE THERE INTERPLANETARY WARS ELSEWHERE IN THE UNIVERSE?

Other beings in the universe are not nearly as warlike as Earthlings, with few exceptions. God is not saying that interplanetary war could never happen, but there has never been a case of beings from one planet fighting with those from another planet. Part of the reason is that once a civilization advances technologically to the point where they could fly warships beyond their own planet, they have also advanced sociologically to the point where they wouldn't. Some beings have moved to other planets, and have even faced resistance from inhabitants of that new planet, but no intelligent beings have ever tried to move to a place where the other beings were so advanced that they could or would fight as equals. Therefore, the imaginings of George Lucas and Gene Roddenberry are more reflective of Earthly attitudes than of any real situation.

182. DOES THE NUMBER 666 MEAN ANYTHING TO YOU?

To God, 666 is just a number. God has more numbers (all the way up to infinity minus one) than you could ever have in a billion lifetimes, and no number gets a better deal than any other number. If you are one of those people who think that some numbers are lucky and other numbers are evil, then you don't really get it, do you?

183. GOD, WHAT WOULD YOU LIKE TO SAY TO THE WORLD TODAY, ESPECIALLY ABOUT THE PROBLEMS, INJUSTICES, AND DIVISIONS THAT ARE SO EVIDENT?

God wants to tell you to wise up. You *may* be lucky enough to survive, as a species, all the insane and unjust acts that you perpetrate or allow your leaders to perpetrate in your name. You *MAY* be lucky enough... but don't count on it. If you want a better life for your children and your grandchildren, indeed, if you want them even to be born, you must take control of your planet, your environment, and your weapons. Too many of you are waiting for God to solve your problems. You invoke God's name as if God were handing out endorsements. God is not coming to your aid. You have the right, the power, and the obligation to make peace on Earth through your own ingenuity and sweat and love for what is good in life.

184. (From "Faxes to God," a series of related questions)

- FOR A MERCIFUL GOD, HAVEN'T YOU BEEN HARD ON THE JEWS?
- IF WE ARE THE CHOSEN PEOPLE, WHY ARE WE MOSTLY CHOSEN FOR HATRED AND ANTI-SEMITISM?
- WHY DID YOU LET HITLER KILL ALL THOSE JEWS IN THE HOLOCAUST?
- I ASK WHY THE HOLOCAUST HAPPENED, AND WHY DID YOU NOT DO ANYTHING ABOUT IT?
- IF YOU HELPED MOSES OUT OF SLAVERY, WHY DIDN'T YOU HELP JEWS IN WORLD WAR II?

Where did you get the idea that God is merciful?

Earth people like to be able to hold someone responsible. It's not your most endearing quality. That's why lawyers get rich. When things go wrong, you want to be able to say, "Okay, we know why." It's human nature to want to blame somebody, to find a reason that your life is not as good as you want it to be. And the favorite scapegoat is God. You believe God is the reason that things go poorly. When the chips are down, people stop thinking of God as the Creator, the ethical judge, and everything else that the Bible portrays God to be. In most people's minds, on a daily basis, God is running the show, God is *culpable*.

"Dammit, *some*body has to have caused this bad thing to happen to me, and if it's not somebody, then it's some*thing*, and that thing makes me mad." Well, to be mad at something, you have to ascribe to that something certain very human characteristics. You blame that thing. You hold it as having human qualities. And if it has human qualities, then it has CHOICE. It had the choice whether to make you have a bad day or allow bad things to occur.

In fact, that's the hope of most people. They want to know that if they do the right thing, or say the right thing – and the right thing might be laying some guilt on God – that the Fates will turn it around, and say, "Okay, let's get fair. Let's balance it out. Let's do something good for this person." And that's what everyone is hoping for. When they pray or when they accuse God of hurting them, they are simply trying to restore some balance or find some good.

God did not create Hitler or Pharaoh or any other bad guys in Earth history. God did not make them evil. God did not make them leaders. You people did that on your own. God did not choose the Jews for suffering. God was powerless to steer events. All God could do was make time pass and things change.

A Press Conference with God

VIII. CULTURE AND SOCIETY
Or, "CULTURE" ALWAYS STARTS WITH "CULT," BUT SOCIETY STARTS WITH YOU

Beyond the desire to understand creation, life, and death, the next thing most people want to know is whether they have chosen well in society, or even if they are among people who have *been* chosen for special treatment. After all, they look around and they see evil people who seem to prosper and good people who struggle and starve. They see people far better off than themselves, and they see other people far worse off. How did this happen? Is all life an accident, or is there a plan, a purpose, a *reason* that some seem luckier and happier than others?

"Culture" seems to define those familiar and (mostly) comfortable aspects of one's life, and the culture with which a person grows up is the one they naturally like the best, from the music they heard regularly to the role models they observed. It's quite natural to want others to like the things you like, which explains the popularity of lists and awards: most popular movie, top 40 hits, best actress, outstanding play, best-selling books, etc. These accolades validate our choices. And what could validate them more than if God likes them, too?

185. CAN YOU MAKE NO ONE HOMELESS OR SICK? *
Unfortunately, no. God is not some all-powerful
social worker. There are so many reasons that people may
be homeless, and so many reasons they may be sick. If God
tried to control all the things that can lead to homelessness
and disease, there would be nothing left for people to enjoy.
Suffering is the price you pay for free will. (See Question
105, Do people have free will?) Indeed, it is the price you
pay for life.

186. WILL I EVER FIND SOMEONE TO LOVE ME?
The most important person who will ever love you
is YOU, for if you do not find yourself lovable, why should
others? If you truly believe you have made yourself the best
person you know how to be, then it is very likely that
someone else will find that goodness in you. Not everyone
shares the same idea of how to be their best, so do not
despair if the first people you meet in your quest for a
companion do not share your vision. They may be looking
for different qualities in a person, or they may be unable to
see your good qualities. Do not try to reinvent yourself for
each person. Remain yourself, your own best self, and love
will come.

However, this question is a curious one to put to
God. Asking it implies either that God might be able to
help you find someone to love you, or that God is a
forecaster of the future, a super-psychic. Neither of these
views of God is correct.

187. WHERE DOES HAPPINESS LIE?

Happiness is different for each person, and it lies in different places and is found in different ways by each person. That which makes you happy might make another person miserable. For example, some people would rather watch ballet than eat. Others would rather eat hemlock than watch ballet.

God is not a Happiness Machine, popping out a different "color" of happiness for each person like some kind of infinite PEZ® Dispenser. The key to happiness is to learn what makes you truly happy and try your best to achieve it. Don't look to others. Don't try to emulate their path to happiness, for it is theirs alone. And don't look to God to make you happy. Your happiness is not God's concern. God is not out to make you miserable, either. Your life is mostly in your hands. Some of the poorest people on Earth are the happiest. Some of the richest are happy, too. Happiness, like disease, will find those who look for and expect it.

188. WHY DO GIRLS NOT LIKE BOYS AND BOYS NOT LIKE GIRLS? *

Girls and boys are still learning how to be people. They do lots of things that grown-ups find cute because grown-ups would never do those things. Later on, the girls will like the boys and the boys will like the girls because they will not be afraid of their friends making fun of them for liking somebody. God does not make the girls and boys fight with each other. They do that all by themselves because they feel funny about liking somebody.

189. SHOULD WE BE TRYING TO PROTECT OUR
ENVIRONMENT, AND IF SO HOW?

The "environment" is not just the resources around you that nourish and sustain you and all other life. It is also the other life itself: the people, animals, and plants. You have not yet evolved – and you may never evolve – to a level at which you can sustain yourselves without all the things that surround you. True, you won't die out as a species just because a particular plant or animal becomes extinct, but you change in minute ways each time that happens. If you put enough of those small changes together, then in time, you Earthlings will change significantly.

The same is true of the resources you extract from your environment. You *will* someday run out of hydrocarbons, particularly oil. You have developed, quite understandably, such a heavy dependence on oil for nearly everything in your life and in your culture, that the end of oil will force unimaginable and unpredictable changes on all Earthlings. Oil, being a naturally occurring substance, will make a comeback on Earth, but it will take millions of years.

Other resources such as air and water will not disappear, but *clean* air and *clean* water could become scarce commodities. Already wars in some parts of the Earth are fought over the rights to control such resources.

You, alone among Earth's animals and other living things, have the ability to control your environment and to interact with others of your species with intelligence and for your mutual benefit. Do not squander this ability.

190. IS GOD A MEMBER OF THE GREEN PARTY?

A member? Heck, God was the FOUNDER, so to speak. God was "green" before green was even a color. Evolution is a very green concept. (See Question 45 about evolution.)

God, of course, not being a person, cannot join any organization, and would not join even if that were possible.

191. WHAT DID GOD THINK OF THE CBS TELEVISION PROGRAM "JOAN OF ARCADIA?"

For those readers unfamiliar with this series, here is a brief description. In the show, God appears to a middle-class white teenager named Joan, and directs her to do certain things without explaining why. God may appear as a black woman in the school cafeteria, a handsome teenage boy, a plumber fixing a leak in Joan's house, or in many other disguises.

In reality, God does not care about this TV program one way or the other, although God thinks it's a healthy sign that Joan regularly says to God things like "You're such a jerk." But the show begs the question whether God can take on human form and appear among you, and as we've said before (see Question 42), the answer is no. Even if God got residuals or a piece of the action in syndication, the answer would still be no.

192. WHAT IS GOD'S FAVORITE SONG?

You Earthlings enjoy songs that sound good to you and resonate with you emotionally, even if it's just to get you dancing. Since God has no hearing and no emotions, God has no favorite song.

Remember, there are "songs" and instruments that can make musical sounds on other planets and other universes. You might not recognize all of these sounds as music, but they are just as much a part of the cosmos.

Now, if you ask me and the rest of the Administration what we like in the way of Earth songs, we'd say we like just about any song with the word "moon" in it, especially if it's combined with something else God created: "Moon Over Miami," "Moonlight in Vermont," "Moon River," and, of course, "That Old Devil Moon." Oh, and yes, "Between the Devil and the Deep Blue Sea" is very nice, especially the way Peggy Lee did it.

We appreciate songs with a good message, like "Jerusalem" by Steve Earle and "Brothers in Arms" by Mark Knopfler and "Let the River Run" by Carly Simon. Songs about God are a problem – too much like worship.

Many songs from other countries and other times are very enjoyable. The ancient Egyptians had a wonderful song, "Kull Ithnan Sawa" which, unfortunately, _no_body sings anymore. And let me say, on those rare occasions when God needs to relax, "Eine Kleine Nachtmusik" is exquisite.

Remember that music is the sound of the cosmos talking. Although the cosmos doesn't provide any lyrics.

193. WHAT ABOUT RAP MUSIC?

Rap music is a precious gift. It is rooted in a form of metered expression that has been used by all people since ancient times. That "volksmusik" has made poetry not only the creation, but also the domain of every person, from the most primitive to the most advanced. Rap is just the rhyme and rhythm of all time set to a modern beat. Of course, none of us can actually stand listening to it.

And speaking of music we don't like, how about "Onward Christian Soldiers." What's up with that? Could anyone have written a more obnoxious song?

194. ARE THERE ANY MOVIES OR TV SHOWS GOD FAVORS?

God knows two important things about visual media. First, you can't make an exciting show about boredom. Second, you cannot make a violent movie and expect it to promote anti-violence.

Movies and television are such new art forms that God has not developed a collection of favorites. God admires that there is such diversity, and that people do not simply try to depict comedy or drama. God is especially fond of nature documentaries, travelogues, anything that shows the diversity of this planet and its species.

195. NAME SOME MOVIES THAT GOD WOULD "LIKE."

Do you work with a computer dating service or something? Are you doing a profile of God for the E! Entertainment channel? Among movies familiar to most Americans that we find have appealing messages are:

2001: A SPACE ODYSSEY, which came very close to revealing universal truths and would have been much better if Keir Dullea had an ounce of acting ability
The first OH, GOD movie
THE NEVERENDING STORY
THE RAPTURE
BEDAZZLED (the 1967 version with Dudley Moore, and Peter Cook as the devil)
Almost any movie with "Green" in the title

196. I'd like to follow up on that list. ARE THERE MOVIES THAT GOD WOULD PROBABLY DISLIKE?

THE NINTH GATE
THE EIGHTH PLANE
THE SEVENTH SIGN (with Demi Moore – just dreadful)
THE SIXTH COMMANDMENT
THE FIFTH ELEMENT
THE FOURTH MAN
THE THIRD SEX
THE SECOND COMING (1975, aka DEAD PEOPLE)
THE FIRST POWER

All of these films have a connection to God or the devil. All are embarrassing. And God doesn't even want to talk about "The Ten Commandments" with Charlton Heston.

197. SO MUCH ART TRIES TO DEPICT GOD OR RELIGIOUS THEMES. WHAT ART IS GOD'S FAVORITE? DOES ANY OF IT GET IT RIGHT?

Graphic arts are a very interesting, human yearning. Earthlings have created images since the very early days. Not all societies on all planets do. You people are *obsessed* with how things _look_. A thing, or even an event, doesn't have to be beautiful for you to be obsessed by it. You often take as much delight in ugliness as you do in beauty. Look at your fascination with car crashes, horror movies, and photographs of war.

But I digress. You asked about religious art. First, none of it "gets it right." It is not possible to depict God, because God has no appearance, and cannot take on any form familiar to you. (See Question 42, Can you take on human form and appear among us?) Not only is it factually wrong to show God as a man, but it is dangerous, as well. It has formed an indelible image in Earthlings' minds of God as a male. Much harm has resulted from that erroneous belief.

God has no favorite artist among Earth people, or, indeed, among any other intelligent beings. God appreciates natural beauty more than anything. That does not mean God is boastful. God did not create the appearance of anything in the universe. It all creates itself in beautiful chaos. Every new universe turns out differently in some ways than any previous universe. Observing that infinite development is the greatest show imaginable.

198. IS "THE DA VINCI CODE" CORRECT? DID JESUS MARRY MARY MAGDALENE? DID THEY HAVE A CHILD? IS THAT HER ON JESUS' RIGHT IN "THE LAST SUPPER?"

We could tell you the real story, but then, you all are having such fun debating and arguing and crying and threatening each other over a *story*, that we really hate to ruin it for you. My goodness, an entire industry spawned by "The Da Vinci Code" would collapse. So, let's just say that no one – not Dan Brown, not the Roman Catholic Church, and certainly not network television – has the whole story correct. Nor, for that matter, do they have the whole story wrong.

You know – you could all be God's daily soap opera, except for one thing. God does not need to be amused. No TV watching for *this* deity.

199. ARE THERE ANY PEOPLE YOU DON'T LIKE?

Anyone who does the tomahawk chop and that Indian war chant.

Once again, we went for the cheap gag first. The cosmos kind of invites that sort of thing. The serious answer is that there are *many* people God dislikes. Actually, "dislikes" is not really an appropriate term. To "like" or "dislike" something implies a human trait. It implies an emotional being. God is not emotional, which, as you know, is a GOOD thing! You would not want something with God's power to be subject to the whims of emotion. The cosmos is chaotic enough without having a manic-depressive at the helm. God is always on an even keel, because God is not just some super-human. God is *nothing like* a human, except for God's sense of humor. Let's just say that God is "inclined" one way or another.

Just because God does not take sides (see Question 175, Whose side are you on in war?), does not mean God is indifferent to all human behavior. God will not intervene to stop _or_ to encourage the behavior of any one person or group of people. That is a really bad idea. Yet God is inclined – there's that word – to see some people as contributing in a positive way to the flow of time and the web of life, and others who contribute in a negative way. The founders of the United States of America were very positive contributors, but not all that followed them have been so magnificent at preserving that dream. In world affairs, there have been many negative influences, such as Attila the Hun, Hitler, and Pol Pot. In culture, there have been those who preserve and honor the past, and those who despoil it. In science, there are people who revel in uncovering another of God's mysteries, and those who then set about using that discovery to destroy God's creations. Destruction is not something God takes lightly. Murder – whether by an individual or by the state – is the worst form of destruction. Murder of a person, by the way, and murder of the environment in which all people survive, are equally offensive to God. Both people and the environment are God's creations. God does not believe one form of destruction is less of a crime than the other.

200. WHO WILL WIN THE NEXT PRESIDENTIAL ELECTION?

Why? Are you thinking of entering? The winner will definitely be the person who gets the most votes. Oh, wait, you better talk to Al Gore about that. You want forecasts? Watch the Weather Channel or call the Psychic Friends. God is not some mystic prognosticator. God has no more idea what will happen in the future than you do.

201. DID GOD GUIDE GEORGE WASHINGTON AND ARRANGE EVENTS TO FORM THE UNITED STATES OF AMERICA?

God has never picked any leader of any group of Earthlings, no matter how small the group, and is not responsible for ANY political divisions of land.

In fact, it's pretty upsetting that you'd even think God would do that. Nothing shows the weakness of Earth people more than the way they create and fight over national boundaries, unless it's the horrible, inept people whom you pick to lead you. Now, to be sure, you have had some wonderful, honest, magnanimous leaders at every level of government. But you've had a lot more stinkers than winners. Don't you think if God were doing the choosing, the results might be a little better? Or do you think that all the good ones were picked by God, after which God couldn't be bothered picking the rest, and so just left it all to chance?

202. DOES ASTROLOGY WORK?

Astrology is very effective at separating gullible people from their money. So it works to help make money for astrologers. Other than that, it's pure Betelgeuse juice.

203. CAN MEDITATION HELP US TO REACH GOD?

No. Forget about "reaching" God. The answers to everything you want to understand about God are not a goal or an end point. You don't reach God the way your airplane finally reaches its destination. There is no trip you can take by just *thinking* hard enough, or by trying to open your mind to the infinite, or through drugs.

204. MANY PEOPLE DO GOOD THINGS IN GOD'S NAME. DOES THAT PLEASE GOD?

No, these people scare God. Well, God does not literally become scared, as in afraid, but God sees these people as going in the wrong direction. The same impulse to do *good* things in the name of God is easily and often misapplied.

Take President George W. Bush. Through his strong faith in God, he believes that God guides his decisions, a belief that is false and dangerous. He absolves himself of guilt or ultimate responsibility for his actions. Sure, the president shares the credit for his more noble acts with God (not that God wants any credit), but Mr. Bush also can easily claim that the bad things he does must, in fact, be GOOD things. That's because he believes God would not abandon him and would not have him do the wrong thing. A person invested with great power or wealth who believes himself to be infallible is the most dangerous person on Earth. People like John Ashcroft think of God the way Popeye thinks of spinach. It makes them feel infallible.

Why not do good things simply because doing good brings greater pleasure and generally a better life to the doer? Why does there have to be a third party – God – in the picture?

201

205. WHAT IMPRESSES GOD MOST – CHARITABLE ACTS OF ATHEISTS OR THOSE OF BELIEVERS HOPING FOR A REWARD?

First, God does not believe in atheists. Second, God is not impressionable. However, God does wonder why there must be a "reward" for good behavior or "punishment" for bad behavior in order for people to do the right thing? By this reasoning, once good people get to heaven, they no longer have any reason to behave themselves, and heaven should be full of obnoxious, ill-behaved angels, while hell should be full of souls who are goody-goodies trying for a "promotion." We've already pointed out that there is no life after death, no heaven for the pure or hell for the wicked. (See Question 119, What is the motivation for people to be good in this life?)

The atheist who behaves "charitably" is not counting on any eternal reward, but still hopes and expects that good behavior will be rewarded in *this* life through greater joy, self-fulfillment, or prestige. The believer who behaves just as well expects a similar reward in this life *and* a further reward after death. The only difference, then, is the size and timing of the anticipated "reward." Is the atheist more "pure" because their "reward" is more temporal? Not really. Is the believer less deserving because they may have acted out of fear of reprisal from God? Of course not. No one is awarded "points" by God based on the reasons for their good behavior. And no "points" are deducted for selfish motivation. God is not some cosmic Santa Claus keeping track of such trivia. Good, charitable behavior is welcome no matter what may be behind it.

206. WHY IS IT THAT SOME PEOPLE SEEM TO HAVE EVERYTHING – GOOD HEALTH, GOOD LOOKS, LOTS OF MONEY, HAPPY LIVES – AND OTHERS SEEM TO HAVE SO LITTLE?

God has noticed that, too. God has also noticed that it tends to be the people who have the easiest lives who complain the most. Mostly they complain about how hard life is. You almost never hear that from the poorest people of the Earth. They are not running off to pet therapists or getting their lips enhanced. It would never occur to them to do that.

207. THEOLOGIAN REINHOLD NIEBUHR WROTE, "MODERN WESTERN CIVILIZATION MAY PERISH BECAUSE IT FALSELY WORSHIPED TECHNOLOGY AS A FINAL GOOD." IS HE CORRECT?

Technology is just technology. It has no soul, no spirit, no past, no future. It is neither inherently good nor inherently bad. Without technology, intelligent beings everywhere in the cosmos would not be able to advance beyond the primitive. Using technology and clamoring for more of it is not worshiping it.

The risk to Earth people comes not from the cult of technology, but rather from *which* technology is nurtured the most. If the technology of killing and destruction and unbridled consumption of resources is the most advanced, then Niebuhr will most likely be correct. If the technology that sustains life and promotes new ways of thinking and traveling and exploring and generating energy gets the most attention, then Niebuhr will most likely be wrong. If the experience of other worlds holds fast, technological advancement may either be your salvation or your doom. God will not decide. You will.

208. WHAT DOES GOD THINK THE DEAL IS WITH GEORGE BUSH AND THE RIGHT-WINGERS?

By definition, the average person has average intelligence. George Bush, though no genius, appears to have slightly above-average intelligence. Therefore, to the average person, he appears smart, and if someone calls him stupid, the average person can't see it AND takes it as an insult to *his or her* intelligence. Average people cannot or will not think through complex problems. They want simple solutions, simply explained.

Explosives strapped to the body of a young person who walks into a restaurant, and explosives strapped to a missile that falls from the sky on a restaurant are both bombs. Both bombs are unexpected; both bombs kill randomly; both bombs are intended to change the political landscape; and both bombs leave the survivors devastated and frightened. That is why hundreds of millions of people cannot see the difference between George Bush and a terrorist. Bombs and fundamentalism are the same thing − simple solutions to complex problems. And that is why George Bush remains popular. "Bring it on." "Let's roll." "You're either with us or against us." Simplicity is the key. In war and in religion, George Bush is a fundamentalist. No doubt, Mr. Bush thinks of himself as a good person, but that does not make him less dangerous. (See Question 149 about fundamentalism.)

Yes, you wish to ask a follow-up question, I see. What do you want to know?

209. PRESIDENT BUSH CLAIMS TO GO TO GOD WITH THE REALLY TOUGH QUESTIONS AND TRIES TO DO GOD'S WILL? HAS GOD SPOKEN WITH HIM OR WITH OTHERS?

Like many people, George W. Bush has spoken TO God, but not WITH God. We think it's just great that so many people turn to God when they have questions or problems. Like everyone else, the President is free to look inside himself, and if thinking he's talking with God helps him, that's fine. But if he deludes himself into thinking that he's been given some authority from God to do what he does, then he is sadly mistaken.

There's nothing wrong with talking TO God to help you sort through a situation. But if you believe that God has talked back, you're just delusional. The things that occur to you during prayer or meditation come from the wellspring of your own mind, not from God.

Here's how you can prove that. Consider that both George W. Bush and Osama bin Laden claim to have an intimate relationship with God, to talk with God, to do God's will. If we assume that both men are sincere in this statement, that neither is lying deliberately, then there are exactly four possibilities that exist.

1) God talks to both George Bush and Osama bin Laden;
2) God talks to George Bush but not to Osama bin Laden;
3) God talks to Osama bin Laden but not to George Bush; or
4) God has never talked to either George Bush or Osama bin Laden.

That's it. There are no other possibilities. Now, which of these scenarios seems most likely? If God talks to both men, then that suggests that God is a pretty ruthless manipulator of life here on Earth, since they are getting very different messages. On the other hand, it would be just as horrific if God were talking only to Bush or only to bin Laden. That kind of favoritism would pretty well doom the human race, wouldn't it? Do you really think that God takes sides, one group against another? It would be mighty hard to take such a God seriously.

But if you believe that God COULD and WOULD take sides, what makes you think it would be the side George Bush is on? Why COULDN'T such a fickle God side with the Muslims instead of the Baptists? After all, both Baptists and Muslims are very devout in their worship and praise of the same God. Both claim to have received God's word telling them how to live their lives. They both believe in Moses and the Ten Commandments. If God were taking sides based just on the fervor of one's beliefs, you've got to believe it would be the Muslims to whom God is more likely to speak.

No, the only possibility that makes any sense is that God is not talking to Bush or bin Laden or anyone else. And if God is not talking to anyone, then any person who says they heard from God is either lying or delusional. Not exactly what you look for in your world leaders, is it?

IX. MORALITY
Or, THERE'S NO BUSINESS LIKE "NO" BUSINESS

There's an old joke that goes like this. The optimist says the glass is half full. The pessimist says the glass is half empty. The pragmatist (or engineer or architect) says the glass is twice as big as it needs to be. This same logic can apply to human behavior. Some people do good things because they hope for a reward. Some people do good things because they hope to avoid punishment. The pragmatist does good things because life itself is better that way.

So many people think of God as the ultimate arbiter of what is Good. Many people want to lead a "good" life. They are motivated by the belief that doing so will yield some kind of reward, first in this life and later in some after-life. The threat of punishment motivates others. "If I weren't afraid of getting caught and going to jail or embarrassing my family, I would steal that money." That, at least, is the Earthly punishment that keeps some people in check. Others fear a more lasting punishment from God.

And so, many questions emerge from these hopes and fears. "If only we knew for sure what is good behavior and what is bad," these questions seem to imply. God does not take that bait. After all, if there were some cosmic list of all the behaviors that earn rewards, it's pretty likely that anything not on the list would never get done.

210. ARE THERE MORAL ABSOLUTES? IS THERE SUCH A THING AS GOOD AND EVIL?

Absolutes? Absolutely not. Even to God, most things are not completely black or white. Good and evil are often relative. What benefits one person frequently harms another. God refrains from taking sides for this very reason, because if God *did* intervene to help someone, another person would suffer.

God cannot read what is in someone's heart or mind, so God is no better at judging a person's actions than any Earthling is. Movies and books would have you believe that God knows everything there is to know, that God sees everything that happens and keeps perfect track of every detail, and that God can read minds and know what each person thinks, cares about, and intends. It's amazing, given all these superpowers, that God has not been turned yet into a comic book superhero! Fortunately for Earth people and intelligent beings everywhere in the universe, God can't do any of those things. That would make God the greatest civil-rights abuser in the history of forever.

Do you really want God with you in the bedroom, or when you're thinking naughty thoughts, or when you're parking in a handicapped spot, or trying to return that new dress you got a spot on? If God *did* read minds, do you think God would just "switch off" whenever your thoughts got too private? How would God know when to start "listening in" again? This mind-reading stuff would pretty much have to be all or nothing. Either God knows *every*thing you think and plan, or God doesn't have a clue about any of it. People who think God knows your thoughts have no idea what that would really involve.

But God is clueless about someone's motives, whether an action was truly evil or just a mistake, whether someone's motives were pure or selfish. Say a soldier kills an unarmed civilian. The witnesses to the event give conflicting stories. Was it murder or self-defense? It would be *nice* to think that there is such a thing as pure justice available, that at least God knows exactly what happened and will someday mete out proper punishment or reward.

Well, forget it. You'll never get God on the witness stand. God cannot see into the soldier's mind or the civilian's heart any better than any person there. Moral absolutes? Not in this cosmos.

211. WHAT, IF ANYTHING, IS A SIN? DO THE
"SEVEN DEADLY SINS" REALLY EXIST?

God did not create the idea of sin. God gave people
free will (see Question 105, Do people have free will?), and
as with all freedom, there is also implied responsibility.
God does not judge what is a sin and who has committed it.

The "seven deadly sins" most assuredly do exist, but
they are not monitored by God. God does not keep a
humongous spreadsheet where each person's sins and
virtues are recorded. "Let's see... Jay Leno has a checkmark
here under 'Lust' last November. We'll have to do
something about *that*."

There's a common vision of God as the ultimate
Morality Cop, a kind of Dirty Harry taking people down
when they step out of line. People think God will sniff out
and punish the naughty, the profane, the boastful, the
greedy. Unfortunately, this vision of God makes God out to
be something of a hypocrite, forbidding killing but blowing
bad people away in ways that Dirty Harry could not begin
to imagine.

For those who can't be bothered looking them up,
the traditional seven deadly sins are anger, envy, gluttony,
greed, lust, pride, and sloth. Mohandas Gandhi had his own
list of seven: wealth without work, pleasure without
conscience, science without humanity, knowledge without
character, politics without principle, commerce without
morality, and worship without sacrifice.

Do you have a follow-up question, or are you just
trying to scratch your elbow?

212. No, I have to follow up what you said, because millions of us want to know, WHAT ABOUT "ORIGINAL SIN?"

Would God be completely out of date by using the term "mastodon droppings?" Earth is the only planet where this concept has come up, which is pretty amazing considering all the planets that support life.

The story of "original sin" would be an amusing little fable if it had not caused so much misery and persecution on Earth. It is an insult to God that people believe God would create a fully grown man and woman, and then, before even one generation goes by, doom all the rest of humanity because these two "failed" some absurd "test" God gave them. If this were the plot of a movie, it would be laughed out of the theatres. NO part of this story makes even the least little bit of sense, and the fact that so many Earthlings believe it is stupefying.

First of all, the biblical story of creation is completely wrong. God did not create Adam and Eve, at least not as two grown adults – or even teenagers – capable of understanding something as complex as language. Why would a force as almighty as God do something so incredibly mean and stupid? Do you honestly believe that God would create these two fertile adults, give them language, and *that's it*⁈? No fire, no clothing, no simple machines, no shelter from the storm. It sounds like a very badly planned game of "Survivor."

Let's back up for a second. According to the Bible, God created all the creatures of the air, sea, and land first. Okay so far. Except, how did those creatures procreate? How did they make new baby creatures? There must have been (and believe me, there were) two sexes of every species. Isn't God supposed to have created fruit trees on the third day, trees that would "bear fruit after their kind?" Yet somehow, when God got around to making humans,

211

God overlooked the fact that he'd need a female? So, the story goes, God created Eve to keep Adam from being "lonely." What kind of girl would that make Eve? (Another downside of this story is that it has been used to make women second-class citizens to this very day.)

Actually, this part of the story is very confusing to God. The book of Genesis says that on the fifth day, God created "man in the image of God, male and female created he them." And, supposedly, "God blessed them: and God said unto them, Be fruitful, and multiply." Who is "them?" Where did "THEY" go? Just a few sentences later, Adam is alone and God is trying to find a "help meet" for Adam. Now, just how was Adam supposed to multiply before Eve came along? "Them" implies there were other people besides Adam, doesn't it? And if they were going to multiply, it sure as a shooting star makes sense that there were already women around before Eve got whipped up.

This story would have you believe that God created everything on Earth, and each time God did a little bit, God sat back, very self-satisfied, and said it was "very good." That's what it says in the Bible. And barely a day later, God says, "It is not good that the man should be alone." So, according to this story, God is either a pretty poor judge of what's good and what's not so good, OR – and this is the key component – God keeps changing God's mind about what is good. This entire story is very confusing and offensive to God, because it says that God, basically, is an on-the-job learner, a tinkerer, blithely making mistakes. It's God as the ultimate micromanager.

If God did not want humans to have knowledge, and in particular, knowledge of "good and evil," why in heck would God have created such a tree, and in the vast lands of all the Earth, placed it right next to Adam and Eve? And how come no one questions that there were talking serpents

212

back then? Not only blessed with intelligence and cunning, but able to speak the same language as Eve.

God understands how such a simple, yet flawed, story first was told. It was made up and shared around campfires by early people with no education, a tiny vocabulary, and absolutely no comprehension of biology, geology, or the size of the Earth. What God cannot understand is why people still believe and tell this story *today*. Surely, even if you are a creationist who rejects all sense of evolution and thinks the Earth is only a few thousand years old, you must recognize that the earliest people had no written language and no scientific knowledge. What makes you think that THOSE are the people to whom God would entrust the secret of creation?

Which brings us back to the question of Original Sin. Now according to the story, God was really ticked off that Adam and Eve had eaten the forbidden fruit and become ashamed that they were naked, which seems like a pretty strange thing to notice first. But okay, let's run with that version. So then, the story tells us, God basically put a curse on Adam and Eve and all their offspring forever, cursing the ground they walk on and making sure that childbirth will be really painful, and they'll eat dust and sweat and die a painful death and then... God gives them each a fur coat! Look it up! How much more absurd does this story have to get before some people realize it's just a story! Original sin? The original sin was how bad this story is!

God does not do things this way. Sure God created the Earth and everything on it. It didn't take six days. It took milliseconds, at least for the creation part. Then it took millions of years for things to settle down and different forms of life to begin from the primordial soup. God was long gone by then, busy creating other universes. Actually,

God was not "gone," as in somewhere else. But God was done fiddling with the Earth. The rest of Earth's natural history took care of itself.

As for the "sin" part, that's another human invention. God does not regulate human behavior. Humans do. (See Question 211 about sin.) God would never create something and then methodically set about destroying it because it didn't "obey" God's rules. God doesn't have rules. There are "laws" in nature, and they're called laws because mere humans cannot willfully break them.

Take it from God – there is no such thing as Original Sin, and no reason to get all hung up on who gets "salvation" and who doesn't. NO ONE gets salvation, at least if you think of salvation as permanent life in "paradise." Every human being starts out with the same chance at a life of pleasure and happiness. There are a lot of factors that get in the way of actually reaping that harvest of joy, but Original Sin is not one of those factors. No one's going to hell just because some woman ate an apple that a serpent told her to eat. Let's get real.

213. HELP US TO KNOW HOW TO LOVE OUR
ENEMIES IN TODAY'S CONFLICT WITH IRAQ AND
OTHER COUNTRIES.

The question you must consider is, who are your enemies? What defines an "enemy?" Certainly, your enemies are not chosen by God. They are chosen by YOU, or by your political leaders, often using the wrong criteria. You think of enemies as someone who hurts you physically or emotionally, yet you don't apply that term "enemy" consistently. You seem to require malice in your enemies. If someone or something hurts you or scares you or depresses you without malice, you accept the injury or insult. Bacteria kill far more of you than any terrorist, but you don't declare war on bacteria, or car accidents, or drownings. Read the next question, too.

214. JESUS TOLD US "LOVE YOUR ENEMIES." WAS HE CRAZY?

Neither crazy nor wrong. Nor the first to say it. But let's face it, Jesus was not the most popular guy in the neighborhood. He came from a very poor family, he hung out with the poorest people, and frankly, his personal hygiene was not the greatest. When people like Jesus walk the streets today – and there are plenty of people just like him – they are cursed, reviled, and ignored. If they are as charismatic as Jesus, they manage to start a small cult. Hundreds of years from now, some of them may even have religions based on their teachings. There are probably people out there crazy enough to start a religion based on this book, but don't bet on it.

Yet for a poor, uneducated outcast, Jesus had a great many insights. Of course, Jesus did not actually say everything attributed to him. Kind of like Yogi Berra. But the point is that Jesus DID come up with the "Love your enemies" line. And it's a great idea. Beings on other planets that truly follow this principle are much more peaceful and much happier.

On the other hand, "love" is a pretty complicated idea (see Question 32, Is it true that God is love?). Jesus did not so much mean to "love" your enemies, as to change them from enemies into friends through thoughtful listening, respect, and diplomacy. Pretty much the same insight the Buddha shared. Buddha and Jesus would have gotten along great if they had known each other. In the days before the printing press and regular trade routes, religious ideas pretty much stayed put in the general area of their birth. So, Jesus never heard of Buddha, who died almost 500 years before Jesus was born.

If Jesus was crazy, so was Buddha. And so are the people today whose good advice is treated with pretty much the same attitude as Jesus' and Buddha's words were in their lifetimes. Genius and goodness are rarely recognized immediately.

215. HOW DOES GOD FEEL ABOUT ABORTION?

First of all, men need to stay entirely out of the debate until they are able to bear children. The intriguing thing about the debate is that it centers on HUMAN life and when it begins, or more specifically around the question, when does a person become a person? Some people feel that if the new life is inside of and drawing its life from the mother, it is not yet a person, that it has no SELF. Others feel life begins with conception. Both sides ignore the fact that humans routinely kill NON-human life to which they play host, by taking antibiotics or using soap or drinking alcohol. To God, all life is the same. God doesn't place a higher value on human life, but understands why you humans DO. God does not control individual destinies. That's why abortion has to be a woman's choice. Rejecting abortion makes a lot of sense, but not for everyone in every situation. Anyone who claims to speak for God on this issue is flat-out lying.

216. So, Jeremiah, you have to answer the follow-up question: WHAT HAPPENS TO THE SOULS OF BABIES THAT ARE ABORTED?

The same thing that happens to every other soul of every other person who dies.

217. DOES GOD SUPPORT CAPITAL PUNISHMENT?

Well, in a sense, God _invented_ it! But I suppose you mean does God think that governments have a right to kill their citizens, and the only possible answer God could give is a resounding NO. If it is wrong for one person to kill another, how can it be right for many people, acting collectively, to kill one? Who gave them that authority? The _impulse_ to kill a bad person is understandable. The _act_ is unforgivable.

218. IS MARRIAGE A GOOD THING? IF SO, WHY?

Marriage is a human invention. (See Question 222, What about premarital sex, etc?) But just because marriage is something you Earth people came up with doesn't make it bad. Far from it. God thinks marriage can be a good idea, though it doesn't always work out. Life is difficult for most people, and as you reach adult age, you realize how very much alone you are in the world. So, it's a wonderful thing to find a companion, someone who likes what you like, and feels what you feel.

Many cultures have arranged marriages. God notes that that tradition began before toothbrushes and toothpaste were invented. God is not saying that an arranged marriage is the only way some people were ever going to find a mate, but does want to point out that arranged marriages pretty much died out in societies where, at the same time, personal hygiene was starting to be important. You do the math.

Many weddings start by saying something like, "We are gathered here in the sight of God...." Don't you believe it. God never watches weddings... or funerals... or any other event for that matter. You may think of your life as one big reality-TV show and that it must be endlessly fascinating, but trust me: God is not sitting back in a recliner with a universal remote control watching everything you do. So, get married because you're in love, and not because God is watching.

219. ARE MARRIAGES MADE IN HEAVEN?

Oh, sure. We have a bunch of yentas sitting around trying to figure out who should marry whom. It's very complicated stuff, matching chromosomes, personality traits, racial biases, etc., and then moving the would-be couple around so that they meet each other under the right circumstances and finally get married. It's a little easier in India and other countries where the marriages are arranged, because we don't have so many things to worry about as we are trying get through the wedding. It's a lot harder getting homosexual couples together because there are so many obstacles we have to overcome.

It can take the yentas years to go through all the eligible people in the annual "Marriage Draft" and arrange all the couples, but it's worth it. After the yentas calculate which two people are going to meet and fall in love, then they turn it over to the "brokers" to get the deal done, manipulating the couple into position. Cinderella's fairy godmother was a broker, one of our best. After the marriage, the couple gets passed to a "monitor" who handles Quality Control. They're the ones who cause divorces. If they see that the couple is NOT a good match, they step in and make the marriage go sour. QC is SO important to heaven.

The answer to your question is, no. And just in case you don't recognize sarcasm when you see it, the previous two paragraphs are total BS. (That stands for "backscatter," not what *you* think it means.)

220. WHY IS MY EX-HUSBAND SUCH A JERK?

Jerks are just part of the natural order, and God does not sit in judgment of who qualifies as a jerk. (See Question 238 about vile people.) Values like "insensitive" or "jerky" are meaningless to God. If your ex is a jerk, it's because he *chooses* to be a jerk. God did not assign him a "Jerk Quotient" (JQ). Even better from your perspective, God did not decree that you'd have to stay with that jerk until death do you part.

221. WHY AM I GAY (HOMOSEXUAL), AND WHY DOES IT MATTER?

How tall are you? You are gay for the same reason you are that tall. It does not matter to God that you are homosexual. So, to whom *does* it matter, and do those people matter to you? God did not make you gay. God did not make other people straight. Sexual orientation is not part of some vast plan. You are not being punished or tested. It just happened.

If you want to know whether sexual orientation is a matter of nature or nurture, I must tell you that the issue is not quite that black and white. The "recipe" is not exactly the same for each person, but in most cases, homosexuality occurs naturally and unavoidably. It's not a choice you were free to make, any more than your straight friends thought about it carefully and "chose" to be straight.

222. WHAT ABOUT PREMARITAL SEX, HOMOSEXUALITY, AND OTHER ISSUES OF MORALITY?

Apparently, you think that God, who refuses to take sides in wars between nations and in debates between religions, is going to care about human rules and foibles. Okay, let's take a deeper look.

Any discussion of premarital sex naturally begs the question of what is meant by "premarital." You're really talking here about sex outside of marriage – "the holy state of matrimony." Where do you people come up with this stuff? The first time God heard that "holy state" business, God just about lost lunch (and that's *definitely* an image you want to avoid). Marriage is a human invention. It's great that two people make an emotional commitment to each other. Life can be hard, and it definitely improves if someone helps you share the burden. But this whole "married in the eyes of God" thing? What can we say to get you to let go of this God-is-watching-you fixation?

You'll notice, by the way, that one of the Seven Commandments that God gave Moses (see Question 152) is "Don't commit adultery." And you might think that means that God is gung-ho on marriage. Wrong. It means God is gung-ho on *honesty*. That's really what ALL the commandments are about. If you're going to make a deep commitment to another person, then you should honor that commitment. You want out? Then GET out. But don't cheat!

Anyway, "premarital sex" is just sex between two people who have not made any kind of commitment to each other. So? Maybe, just maybe, because they have sex, they'll decide to make such a commitment. Sure it's a long shot. So's the lottery, and yet millions of people buy a ticket every day. So, take a chance on love. Basically, you humans

221

are just animals anyway, and sex (which means different things to different species) is an instinct for most animals.

Now, of course, when we talk about sex, we're also talking about procreation, the urge of the species to sustain itself. God is aware that some people think that sex must exist only for that purpose, and that any form of sex that does not allow for the possibility of procreation is wrong. We are fascinated by the multitude of ideas that Earth people come up with. This concept of sex did not come from God, and it's definitely *not* part of your genetic make-up.

Even if sex were just for procreation, that would not preclude sex outside of the marriage commitment, as WAY too many young people have found out. When Earthlings complain about sex between unmarried people, they are really concerned about something other than procreation, and God wants me to talk about morality in general in a minute.

But first, God wants to polish off this procreation debate. Sustaining a species is important, but it's not all there is to life. You don't get points with God for being a great procreator. (And even if you did get "points," what would you trade them in for, anyway?) Life does not exist for some ultimate purpose. It just exists. Across the cosmos, living things in billions of species manage to sustain themselves without "rules" like marriage and sexual abstinence. In fact, most species right here on Earth do just fine, even though they may engage in "sexual" activities (like dropping seeds) that have no chance of procreating *any*thing.

No, it seems to God that the rules about sex are designed by Earthlings for one reason only: to prevent pleasure. Frankly, God cannot understand that obsession so many humans have. What good is having life if you won't take pleasure in all that accompanies it? Yet, rule after rule does nothing more than eliminate pleasure or make someone feel bad for experiencing it. Species throughout the cosmos seek and take pleasure in life. Flowers turn to get the full pleasure of the sun's rays. Dogs delight in catching things that fall. Birds drop their stuff on windshields. None of these things are necessary to sustain life. They are experiences of pleasure for the sake of pleasure, for the sake of reveling in LIFE. There's no master plan to life. God did not create everything for some grand purpose. Those things that will make a life pleasurable are there because God wants all life to BE pleasurable. If God thought sex should be proscribed, it would not be nearly as much fun as it can be.

Which brings us right back to love. God has no problem with homosexuality. If it were "unnatural," it would not exist so naturally throughout millions of species. God believes that the same rules should apply to homosexual relationships as to all others. And guess what? It's what you Earth people call The Golden Rule. If something you do gives another person pleasure and does not harm them in any way, it should be okay. God finds absolutely nothing wrong in giving and receiving pleasure for its own sake, for that is when people – and other species – feel most alive, as long as both people are old enough to give *informed* consent. Love (not to be confused with sex) between two people – ANY two people – is a beautiful thing that celebrates God's creation. For sex to promote love, it must be consensual, and that's where we get back into issues of morality.

Morality is fine when it supports and affirms life and prevents one person from harming another physically or emotionally. Morality has no place when it is used solely to deny pleasure to another person. There are people who *don't* find pleasure in sex or certain other behaviors. Those people are doing the right thing to avoid such activities. But they have no right to force their notion of pleasure on anyone else.

223. DID GOD CREATE AIDS AS A WAY TO REDUCE HOMOSEXUALITY? WHAT IS GOD'S POSITION ON GAY MARRIAGE?

You're kidding with that first question, right? You realize that by asking it, you're allying yourself with great minds such as Jerry Falwell and Moammar Khadafi. (If God were looking for a way to reduce people, God might start by reducing Falwell and Khadafi. Fortunately for them, God has no such agenda.)

Are you afraid that life isn't hard enough already for gay men? That it's so carefree a life that God would decide to make it harder, and even kill people to make a point? You really must stop thinking of God like some character in a Dickens novel. That's a pretty cruel and, dare I say, unimaginative God you have there. Surely this God you've dreamed up could find something better than death to alter human behavior. If you think that God can create new viruses and use them mostly to attack and kill gay men, then is it such a stretch to think that God could, oh, I don't know, make grass grow on their heads instead of hair? Wouldn't that be just as effective? Gay men wouldn't die; they'd just have to get their hair cut twice a week. That would probably be an even more effective deterrent.

The hypocrisy about gays among religious denominations is incredible. So many people want to believe that God is responsible for all the things they _like_ in life, and that everything else somehow just happened while God wasn't looking. They will refer to a very talented person – a dancer, perhaps, or an athlete, or a composer – as having a "gift from God." Yet if that person happens to be homosexual, somehow that component of the person is an aberration. This kind of narrow-minded thinking is an insult to God. It suggests that God is incapable of getting the whole package right, like some computer programmer who overlooks a really glaring bug. If God DID invest an individual person with particular skills and personality traits, don't you think God would also determine that person's sexuality, rather than leave it to chance?

Of course, God does NOT make or control each person or *any* person. Homosexuality is neither a gift nor a curse from God. Each of you is on your own. You are free to love whomever you choose.

Love between *truly* consenting adults can never be wrong, no matter how that love is expressed. (Forced consent doesn't count.) Since marriage is a human institution, humans get to decide who can be married. We find it curious that two gay people should be denied the right to marry, but as with all things human, God is staying out of it.

224. I'M CURIOUS HOW OUR DEFINITION OF LOVE, PARTICULARLY ROMANTIC LOVE, IS EVOLVING ALONG WITH EVERYTHING ELSE. SOCIETY PLACES RESTRAINTS ON WHOM WE CAN LOVE AND HOW MANY PEOPLE WE CAN LOVE. WE ARE TAUGHT VERY EARLY THAT MONOGAMY IS KING, MATES SHOULD BE ABOUT THE SAME AGE, AND SO ON. ARE WE MOVING TOWARD A FREER ATTITUDE ABOUT LOVE AND AWAY FROM PETTY JEALOUSY, POSSESSIVENESS, AND A VERY LIMITING VIEW OF HOW TO LOVE?

The Living Things Control Officer (LTCO) back with God's Support Staff wants to know if you are busy after the Press Conference.

Okay, no need to get agitated; that was just a joke. You are definitely NOT the LTCO's "type," so don't worry. But, to get serious for at least the next ten seconds, love is surely evolving on many levels. The power of the human brain is much greater now than at any time in your history. All the cute "I ♥ New York" bumper stickers to the contrary, love resides in the brain. The rules by which you choose to live are also constantly changing, as they must to accommodate all the new knowledge you develop and share. This combination of physical evolution and societal evolution continually redefines "love." If your future follows other planets' patterns, many of your attitudes about love will also change towards greater freedom.

You might not want to count on possessiveness ever entirely going away. Next question.

225.   WHY ARE PEOPLE SO GREEDY?

Why pick on greed? What about pride or sloth, or my personal favorite, lust? (See Question 211 on the Seven Deadly Sins.) God does not speculate on human behavior. God has no frame of reference for understanding anything you people do. God does not control your actions or your personalities. Most living things on Earth and on other planets do not exhibit greedy behavior. Maybe it's something in your water.

226. IS HONESTY WORTH ALL THE FLAK WE HAVE TO TAKE FOR IT?

Why ask God? You're not getting any flak from God, whether you are honest or not. God recommends that your life will be better if you are honest with yourself and honest in most dealings with others. The so-called Golden Rule − behave towards others as you would have them behave towards you − is accepted among all intelligent beings in the cosmos. Honesty may not always be rewarded, but your odds of enjoying life improve greatly if you are honest.

227. DOES GOD CONDONE CLONING?

Condone it? God does not condone anything, or, for that matter, endorse anything. People who want forgiveness for things they've done wrong or a "sign" of the things they should do are mistaking God for a meddling cleric.

God sees cloning as just another step on the natural path of technological evolution. It's part of the same instinct that leads some Earth people to forbid contraception and abortion. It is, as Kahlil Gibran called it, "Life's longing for itself." Beings on other planets have perfected cloning, and they are able to use it to reduce disease, eliminate concerns about infertility, and advance their society. Given all the benefits of cloning, it's easy to see why your "leaders" want to restrict it.

228. IS GOD WATCHING WHEN WE DO THINGS, ESPECIALLY THINGS WE SHOULD NOT BE DOING?

No, God is not "watching" in the way that Earth people think of this word. God does not have eyes. God is not a camera, secretly recording everything. God is all things, everywhere, but only in the present moment. So when something – anything – occurs, it impacts the present and causes a change that manifests itself in the next moment. Most events have very tiny impacts. Like blinking your eyes, or taking a breath, or turning your head. Yet even these small events send out ripples. For example, each time you breath in, you inhale millions of particles and microscopic animals. What for you is the most trivial of acts is, for them, their whole lives. Oxygen is changed to carbon dioxide. The ripples from most changes do not extend very far, but some events send out ripples that effect more change, and more change from that. God does not monitor and record every change, like some almighty Big Brother. But because God is IN every thing, God is affected BY every thing.

As far as things you "should not be doing," you should be much more afraid of how you hurt yourselves and everyone around you, than whether you're going to get in trouble with some invisible overlord. You should do the right thing *because* it's the right thing, not because of fear of retribution, at least not from God. God does not control what humans think or do, what kind of art they create or words they speak. God is not like some Ozark preacher running around tearing down offensive images.

229. WHY IS THE SEX ACT, WHICH IS ONE OF THE MOST NATURAL THINGS IN THE WORLD, CONSIDERED SO TABOO BY MOST PEOPLE?

Whoa, let's see if God can beat the buzzer on that one. Tick. Tick. Tick. (BUZZZZZ!) Beats God.

The key word here is "most" people. That means that there are some intelligent beings in the cosmos, some of whom are right here on Earth, who have no taboos about sex. They do treat it as something very natural and make virtually no rules that put limitations on it.

Remember! Not all intelligent beings everywhere have to be the same. Judging from your movies and your TV shows, you pretty much have accepted that other beings would not look like you. Even those who live on Earth are expected to look "different," to have a "primitive" appearance. Well, if they don't all have to _look like_ you Earthlings, why do they have to have the same emotions as you? Why do you think their lifespan would equal humans'? Aren't many of your rules based on your lifespan? Of course they are! Look at your species' rule against child pornography. You set an age limit for sex between a younger person and an older, supposedly more mature, person. That's a very good rule for you humans, because you have learned that such sex is not healthy for the "under-aged" person.

But suppose you humans lived only to age 35, and your children were sexually mature at age 10, and anyone over 30 would age quickly. Would you still make the "age of consent" 18? Not likely. You'd lower it.

Now, let's say you Earth people, with your taboos, happen to run into that species, one very close to your own in terms of DNA, that has no taboos, no rules regarding sex, and you see a 28-year-old male about to have sex with a 12-year-old female. She is not upset. In fact, they don't even mind that you are watching. Your presence is neither stimulating nor distracting. You are no more significant than the furniture or ground (or air) on which they mate. What do you do? With your training as an Earth person, what do you do? Are you shocked? Do you try to stop it? Do you look away and flee? Do you tell them afterwards that what they did was wrong? Do you feel a compulsion to protect the young female?

Why? Why would you? If you are in *their* culture, you do not stop them. If *they* are in *your* culture, then you may have a right to explain the rules here to them, without punishing them for following *their* natural instincts.

And when you get right down to it, aren't all taboos the same, whether they are about sexual behavior or any *other* kind of behavior? Taboos exist because a society will always try to do what it thinks it must do to survive *as* a society. Intelligent beings everywhere are coded pretty much the same way, to evolve in body *and in mind* to the point where self-preservation is assured. It is not enough only that the body evolves efficiently. The intellect and the culture it creates must also evolve new ways of thinking. Only when that happens on Earth – and it has not finished happening yet, to judge by other planets – will Earth people have a chance of avoiding annihilation someday, perhaps uncountable years from now.

So, *accept* your taboos, and change them from time to time as conditions warrant, for you will probably not be the same society in 500 years that you are today.

230. IS GOD CONCERNED BY BLASPHEMY? WHAT
DO YOU CONSIDER BLASPHEMOUS?
    You mean like this book?

It is not possible to offend God. If it *were* possible,
mere words would not do it. True blasphemy – the act of
showing disrespect to God – comes in damage to the
environment, in killing animals and plants and other people
for no good reason. (Good reasons include eating and
protecting others from destruction.) Children understand
this distinction. They say, "Sticks and stones may break my
bones, but names will never hurt me." That goes double for
God. Most people who are concerned or offended by
blasphemous speech are substituting their own feelings for
God, which is arrogant and foolish. If God is not offended
by even careless words, why should *they* be? People who
know better but who still persist in destroying God's
creations are much worse than someone who merely uses
words, however thoughtlessly.

A Press Conference with God

X. HUMANITY
Or, IT'S NOT THE HEAT, IT'S THE HUMANITY

Nothing is more fascinating to us humans than our own humanness. We find ourselves endlessly fascinating, and assume that God must find us equally wonderful and, therefore, favor us above all other creations, living and non-living. And if God likes us, really, really likes us, then wouldn't God also like some of us better than others? Let's find out!

231. DOES GOD HAVE A FAVORITE PEOPLE OR A FAVORITE *TYPE* OF PERSON?

Ah, you are making an assumption here about the nature of God. You are assuming that God has emotions, that God likes some of God's creations more than others. Isn't *that* a scary thought? What criteria would God use to decide on a favorite person or tribe or anything? Some people think they know the criteria that God uses, and they use that supposed knowledge to hate and destroy the people and the things that THEY think God hates. What arrogance these people have, to think they totally understand God, and that God would reveal certain truths only to THEM. (See Question 242 about God blessing things.) There is nothing wrong with wanting good things to come to you and your friends and your environment. It's natural to want that. Just don't expect God to take sides or protect you. (See Question 175, Whose side are you on in war?)

232. MY DEAR CHILD: YOU ARE IN HEAVEN NOW
AND DO NOT HAVE TO SEE THE EVILS THAT MAN
IS DOING TO THE CHILDREN. THE CHILDREN
ARE SUFFERING SO BADLY, EVERY DAY NEW
CHILDREN ARE LEAVING – POLLY FROM
PETALUMA, THE LITTLE GIRL FROM MISSOURI,
AND ALL THE OTHERS THAT WERE HURT AND
SUFFERED. WHY IS LIFE SO HARD FOR
AMERICA'S CHILDREN? WHY DOES GOD ALLOW
THEM TO SUFFER? *

It's not just America's children who suffer. In fact,
life is much harder for children from other countries where
they face starvation, disease, lack of education, PLUS all the
bad things that get visited on American boys and girls.

So, isn't it comforting to know that God does NOT
control things? Which of the following scenarios would
bring you more comfort?

a) Living in a world where an all-powerful
being can create suffering and there's
nothing you can do about it?

b) Living in a world in which an all-powerful
being could *prevent* suffering but chooses not
to and allows it to continue, or randomly
decides which problems to fix?

c) Living in a world where bad things just
happen and people can act to prevent them?

If you chose "c," you chose wisely. Evil and
suffering do not come from God, and God does not hold the
answer. You do. People must work together to make life
better for the children AND for the adults, safe in the
knowledge that God will not capriciously undo your hard
work.

233. WHAT SHOULD WE DO, IF ANYTHING, ABOUT OVERPOPULATION?

Stop doing it! Find what's causing it and stop! Is that so hard to figure out? God knows that there are many Earth people who don't see overpopulation as a problem. God does not do predictions, so don't expect God to be able to tell you when or if Earth's "population bomb" is going to go off. And if it never goes off, does that mean it wasn't a bomb?

Based on the experience of other planets with similar anthropological backgrounds, it seems likely that humanity ultimately will destroy itself, or most of itself, *if* nothing is done about population growth. Your choice is to prevent people from being born, or watch them die a miserable, young death. The Earth's resources are not infinite. Again, God is looking at planets of a comparable size and solar system.

Other planets similar to Earth have found that, before they learned how to tap the resources of nearby celestial bodies that were not being used to support life, they exhausted most of the resources on their own planet. Then, many species of life disappeared for several million years, until a new form of intelligent life evolved to a point of sustaining itself. The reason it took several million years is that the planet needed time to renew its own ecosystem, building up new fossil fuels, purifying its soil and water, and adjusting its climate accordingly. Also, the evolution of species from the primordial ooze takes a long time.

Which brings us back to overpopulation. The other common result of too many people on planets similar to Earth has been massive war. God doesn't care how much intelligence you have, you are still going to get territorial and aggressive when you find yourself running short of the resources needed to sustain life.

Thus, the Middle East will most likely always experience war. Ultimately, though, it will be only about water, and not about religion or oil. Those who have water and who have the means to control its flow will find themselves both revered and hated. Nearby areas that have no water will beg and plead for more and more water. When they get more water, their population will grow. So, then they will need *more* water. The day will come when the level of need surpasses the supply. (You Earthlings already see this often in Africa.) Then those who have the water can expect those who don't to ask less politely, and then to demand, and then to attack. That is the usual sequence of events. The only solution to prevent it is to reduce voluntarily the number of new people created. If couples would have no more than two children, the Earth could sustain itself for many, many more years than if the population is allowed to grow unchecked.

The population bomb is similar in structure to the "corporation bomb," but in reverse. Many companies are built on the premise that they must continually grow larger in order to survive. If they just stay the same size, eventually they will begin to shrink and die. Yet, the solution is to expand and put off dying for many years. Since nothing can grow forever, those businesses that depend on growth tend to burn out quickly when they can no longer grow. Then the resources of that once-great company are distributed to the upstarts that haven't yet made all the mistakes. The business world renews itself in this fashion, and so does the natural world.

Of course, all of this kind of growth control ultimately, billions of years from now, will still not prevent your sun from expanding in its death throes and incinerating the entire solar system. But that's part of the lifecycle of the cosmos, too.

234. IS IT OKAY TO USE CONTRACEPTIVES TO CONTROL BIRTH RATES?

God doesn't play the game, so God doesn't make the rules. If that's what you want to do to prevent overpopulation, go right ahead. God does not disapprove.

235. DOES HUMANKIND LEARN FROM ITS MISTAKES?

It hasn't yet, has it? People, and especially their governments both elected and unelected, continue to make the same mistakes. Only the technologies change. Yet the mentality behind the mistakes remains the same. In some societies on other planets, the intelligent beings eventually evolve beyond the jealousy and greed that underlies most mistakes. It could yet happen on Earth.

236. WHAT SHOULD HUMANS' RELATIONSHIP TO OTHER CREATURES ON EARTH BE? SHOULD WE EAT THEM? SHOULD WE MAKE THEM WORK FOR US? SHOULD WE HAVE THEM AS PETS? IN OTHER WORDS, HOW DO YOU SEE US VIS-À-VIS YOUR OTHER CREATURES?

You're doing just fine, most of the time. The only time you err is when you kill creatures for absolutely no reason. (See Question 174 about killing bugs and Question 95 about killing for sport.) There is no right way or wrong way to be a human inhabitant of Earth. You do what you do, not because you are *supposed* to do that, but because it comes naturally. God does not favor one creation over another. To God, you are no better than a beet, no worse than a worm. If some of you use animals for food, and others use the same animals for companionship, it's of no consequence to God. One animal eats another. Whose side should God be on? The carnivore lives only because the other animal dies. Should the carnivore die for lack of food? (See Question 67 about contact with other intelligent beings.)

237. HOW IS IT THAT SO OFTEN I DO HARM THAT
I DO NOT MEAN TO DO, AND I FAIL TO DO THE
GOOD THINGS I INTEND? EVERY DAY, WE
BETRAY OURSELVES. WE BREAK OUR OWN
RULES, AND WE DELIBERATELY SAY THINGS,
THINK THINGS, OR DO THINGS OF WHICH WE
ARE ASHAMED OR THAT MAKE US UNHAPPY.
SOMETIMES – AS WITH ALCOHOL, TOBACCO, SEX,
AMBITIONS, OR SELFISHNESS – WE EVEN
DESTROY OURSELVES. WHY DO WE NOT RESIST
THESE TEMPTATIONS THAT CAUSE US TO DENY
ALL THAT WE BELIEVE IN, EVEN LEADING US TO
HURT OUR LOVED ONES AND OUR FRIENDS? ON
THE OTHER HAND, WHY ARE WE OFTEN UNABLE
TO ACCOMPLISH THE GOOD THINGS WE WISH TO
DO?

God, as we have noted often in this book, is not a
mind reader. God does not monitor your thoughts or even
your actions, and that's a good thing. Yet, God observes
the human condition and marvels at the ways in which it
manifests itself.

Life on Earth is a series of surprises, barely
controlled chaos that masquerades as reason and order.
One moment a chipmunk scampers across a field; the next
moment it is a meal for a hawk. A flower grows and
suddenly its pollen is stripped by a bee or blown by the
wind. The fact that new life may come from this assault
does not mask its chaotic nature.

Earth people, alone among the living things on
Earth, try to hide from and distort the chaos that is inherent
in nature and in life. Even the "rules" you set for yourself
are often at odds with the animals you are. That's not a bad
thing, because it is through the development of rules and
new ways of respecting them that you advance as a species.

But rules create an inherent conflict between your natural being and the being you aspire to become.

In almost every case, the rules fall apart when confronted with people's desire for pleasure. That is why the most rigid of you are so adamantly opposed to pleasure, why so many rules are designed to subvert it. Such rules will always fail because of Earthlings' undeniable quest to be pleased. And, of course, that is why people fantasized the traditional version of God, because people want someone to *be* pleased *for* them. Even if no one else notices, even if no one else cares, the traditional belief is that "God cares." That belief, false as it is, allows people to feel pride and take pleasure.

Most Earth people have a pretty strong sense of what is good – meaning acceptable – behavior, and what is bad, or unacceptable. Yet, the rules are often in conflict with the desire. Sexual desire, in particular, has the power to overcome the inhibitions placed in the mind by the rules. One part of the mind betrays the other. If no one is harmed by the betrayal, then the person rationalizes it, and may continue the betrayal. In virtually every case, there is a quest for pleasure involved, which may be sexual pleasure or some material gain. The person may feel badly for what they are doing, but they won't stop until they are "caught," which typically means until someone they care about is hurt by what they do.

God is not the Steven Spielberg directing this movie. Each person has free will (see Question 105, Do people have free will?), and that means you have the freedom to be a jerk. Those who wait for God to straighten them out are the ones most likely to keep giving in to temptation or failing to do the good things they intend to do. Those who realize that God will not intervene to make them better, understand that they must take personal responsibility to be the person they wish to be.

Remember, doing that which is hard for you to do is, most likely, the exact thing you should be doing (as long as no one else gets hurt, physically or emotionally).

238. WHY DOES GOD LET VILE PEOPLE PROCREATE?

It's funny, but the vile people asked the same question about *you*. Vile people are just part of the natural order, and God does not sit in judgment of who qualifies as vile or who gets to procreate. Values like "vile" or "friendly" are meaningless to God. In any event, God does not "let" people do anything, any more than God "makes" people do things. God does not control human behavior. In terms of procreation, God is not running some sort of fertility clinic, sorting out who gets pregnant and who does not. Anyone who is unable to procreate can take comfort in knowing that they are not being punished by God. On the other hand, those who can pop out babies like a vending machine pops out breath mints should not consider that as some sign that God likes them better.

239. HOW DOES GOD FEEL ABOUT PROSPECTIVE PARENTS TRYING TO CHOOSE THE SEX OF THEIR CHILDREN?

God does not choose or set the gender of a child at the moment of conception. YOU choose it, or more specifically, the male seed chooses it. That this choice has always been random and beyond *your* ability to make a conscious, deliberate selection does not change the fact that God was not involved. Therefore, if you learn how to pre-select a baby's gender at conception (and not a moment later) and wish to use this knowledge, you are not playing God. You are playing Earthling, the Upgrade Version.

240. MY LOVE IS EVERYTHING FOR ME.
NOTHING HAS MORE VALUE FOR ME THAN
THOSE I LOVE. WHEN EVERYTHING WILL HAVE
DISAPPEARED, LORD, WHO WILL REMEMBER THE
VALUE OF THAT LOVE? DOES LOVE HAVE
VALUE?

Like so many other terms we've discussed in this book, "value" is relative. What is value? It is a meaningless term to God, but God knows it is a useful term to people. A thing has value if it is used to some purpose, and no value at all if it is never used. Emotions exist only in the mind, which is the same place a sense of value exists. So, if you perceive something to have value to you, then it does.

The food you ate this morning existed before you ate it. In consuming it, you changed it and derived value from it. But in your extracting that value, you changed the food. It no longer exists in its previous form. It is but a memory, and a fleeting one at that. It changed you in some minute way, gave you energy or strength, helped your body to survive, perhaps even gave you pleasure. Who remembers the value of that food? Will you still remember it a month from now? A year? Ten years? Of course not. Yet it had value, and through its helping make you the living person you are today, it had some lasting value. Love is like that food, except you can both receive it and give it.

Something need not be permanent itself to be of value. You yourself are of value to those who know you. Eventually, the memory of you will pass from the Earth, yet you will have left some permanent change in your place.

241. IT SEEMS THAT PEOPLE NO LONGER GET WORKED UP OVER BIG CAUSES. DOES THAT MEAN WE HAVE ALREADY EVOLVED AS A PEOPLE TO THE POINT WHERE THERE ARE NO MAJOR BATTLES TO FIGHT, LIKE ENDING SLAVERY AND ESTABLISHING HUMAN RIGHTS FOR ALL THE PEOPLE OF THE WORLD?

No Big Causes? How about the cause of evolution itself? God, the creator, gave you evolution, but many people want to deny it exists. The "creationists" want to believe that God created everything with a master plan for all eternity, and that absolutely nothing changes, because God is perfect, except that if things DO change, it's because God wanted to improve on perfection. None of which makes much sense, does it?

242. HOW DOES GOD REACT WHEN SOMEONE SAYS, "GOD BLESS" SOMETHING?

God is not in the business of blessing things. In fact, God does not even know what that means. What are people asking of God? Do they understand the full measure of their request, or has blessing things become perfunctory? For most people, asking God's blessing on something has become a cliché, an entreaty that has no real meaning, or, perhaps, too *many* meanings.

For example, when someone says, "God Bless America," they may be asking for different things. They may want God simply to protect America from harm. Or they may want God to reward America in some way. Or they may want God to favor America, take her side. Or all of the above.

God is very concerned (as you know from other answers in this book) with the arrogant nature of Earth people. You expect God to be something God is not. You expect God to be sometimes like each of the following:

- a servant, here to make things you wish for come true
- a magician, putting on a show for your amusement
- a dictator, at turns benevolent and cruel.
- an inventor, an architect, and a builder all in one, whipping up new planets and species at will

God is NONE of those things. God DOES none of those things. God is not there for you to command or beseech. God is God, beyond all imagination.

So, when you ask God's blessing, you are engaging in superstitious, wishful thinking. You are saying, "I don't know what's out there, but I sure hope it speaks my language, and just happens to be listening, and will do something that I think would be good." It's kind of quaint, actually. But it's also insulting to God and terribly arrogant, because most of the time when you ask for God's blessing on one thing, you are secretly hoping that God will take sides against something else. "God Bless America" sometimes means "God Protect America from harm," but it just as often means "God, do something bad to the people we don't like."

Sorting out all the requested blessings is not God's "thing." There is nothing wrong with wanting good things to come to you and your friends and your environment. It's natural to want that. Just don't expect God to take sides or protect you. They say, "The Lord helps those who help themselves," and that's good advice, even though "the Lord" won't technically be giving any direct help. (Even now, as you read this, we can tell that most of you are still thinking of God as a man.)

243. DOES GOD ACTUALLY "DAMN" PEOPLE?

There are two parts to this answer. The first part is the same as the question about God blessing people. God does not play requests. God won't bless or damn something just because someone asks.

The second part is a bit more interesting. Most humans think of God as a being with unlimited intelligence, unlimited power, and unlimited interest in what happens in their lives and in all existence, living or inanimate. Naturally, a being with that kind of nature would be expected to "fix the horse race," so to speak, to make decisions about what happens in the universe. It's still the same misunderstanding of what God is and what God does.

God is not like some character in a Damon Runyon play. God does not go through mood swings, or make "good" things happen *here* and "bad" things happen *there*. God does not control things in order to make some predetermined result take place. And it's a good thing for you that God does not intervene! The laws of physics that make everything "work" together would likely be subjected to some rather wild fluctuations if God were the kind of being most humans imagine. There is enough randomness in the cosmos without a capricious and temper-tantrum-toting God getting involved. In other words, God does not play God. God is not some super-engineer treating the Earth like some giant model-train set, throwing switches like crazy just to watch two trains collide or another train fling itself off the tracks.

So, no, God does not damn anything. That would be a pretty rotten trick, and God is not a rotten trickster.

244. NATURE SHOWS THAT THE PREDATOR
FEEDS OFF ITS VICTIM, THAT AMONG ANIMALS
THERE IS NO CHARITY – THE STRONG DOMINATE
THE WEAK. THAT IS ESSENTIALLY WHAT
HITLER SAID, THAT THE EARTH BELONGS TO
THE STRONG. WAS HE WRONG?

It is not possible to say that Hitler was right about anything without someone taking offense, so this question puts your humble Press Secretary at risk.

Can you tell I'm procrastinating on answering?

Hitler was no anthropologist. Yet Hitler knew how to exploit the fact that many people respect only strength, and respond well when they feel they are in harm's way, when they are afraid. So, Hitler declared that the Homeland was in danger from so many enemies. He was able to raise an army that believed, ultimately, that it was proper for them to attack and kill other tribes of people. (For that is what your country divisions are. Pride in nationality is not defined as much by artificial *country borders* as it by ancient tribal connections.) And so Hitler's tribe of citizens fought a war they thought they were right to start. (Doesn't this sound familiar?)

In many ways, you could say that Hitler himself figured out a way for the weak – and Hitler WAS weak – to dominate the strong. This horrible, puny, mentally sick man was able to calculate that Germans – and remember that Hitler was NOT German-born – believed that the strong must dominate the weak. He turned the might of a nation to his aims, and got people to die for the ideas he helped plant in their minds. The unspeakable evil Hitler wrought, he wrought on all humanity.

So, perhaps, Hitler helped prove that at a certain point, the mind has to evolve to catch up with the body. If

250

Hitler's adopted tribe had picked up on how he was lying and exploiting them, Hitler the Weak could not have succeeded. Unfortunately, in just 60 years since Hitler's time, humans have not evolved very much on that front. Evil exploiters like Hitler will come along many more times on Earth before the common intellect of Earth people is ready to recognize them for what they are.

245. YOU KNOW THAT SAYING THAT GOES SOMETHING LIKE, "GOD NEVER GIVES US MORE TROUBLE THAN WE CAN HANDLE." PLEASE EXPLAIN. AND ABOUT THAT "HOW MUCH WE CAN HANDLE" PART – WHY HAS GOD TESTED MY LIMITS SO RIGOROUSLY? SURELY, OUR PERCEPTIONS ON MY CAPACITY DIFFER VASTLY!

Well, we have bad news and good news. Neither trouble nor its solution comes from God. The bad news is, you're on your own. The GOOD news is, you're on your own. (See the next question and Question 232 about why children suffer.) Surely, it is a comfort to you to know that you have not been secretly selected for strife. You are not the unknowing and nonconsenting subject of some test of your limits to endure pain and heartbreak. Perhaps you've had more than your fair share of trouble, but if you DO manage to handle it, you can be confident that no one is plotting to undo your hard work. You must not withdraw from life because you are frustrated, but put yourself in the path of the good luck that will eventually come your way.

246. WHEN I HAVE A SERIOUS PROBLEM IN MY
LIFE THAT I CAN'T QUITE FIX, SHOULD I JUST
GIVE UP AND SAY "IT'S IN GOD'S HANDS NOW," OR
SHOULD I KEEP TRYING UNTIL I HAVE A
NERVOUS BREAKDOWN?

Don't put your life in God's hands. For one thing,
God has no hands and cannot catch you as you fall. Those
people who relinquish control of their lives are really trying
to absolve themselves of responsibility. You have incredible
power. Some people in the depths of despair seek a "higher
power," yet they fail to realize that this higher power is
inside each Earthling already. Lots of people who could use
help worry that they may have flubbed their chance, that
they are not "worthy" to be helped. God wants them to
know that they have nothing to worry about. You, like
nearly everyone, already possess the power to help yourself.
You are not being punished or tested. The cosmos is ready
for you, and even more importantly, *you* are ready for it!
(See the previous question.)

247. MANY PEOPLE PUT THEIR FAITH, HOPE, AND DREAMS IN A MERCIFUL GOD, A THINKING GOD, A GOD LIKE THE GOD OF THE BIBLE. IF GOD IS NOT THAT KIND OF GOD, WHAT SHOULD THEY DO NOW?

The answer from God is not unlike the answer Dorothy received when she thought she was trapped in Oz and all hope was gone. The Good Witch told her that she had always had the power to return home whenever she wanted.

And so it is with you Earth people. You have always had the ability to make your own lives better, to find the love you desire and the happiness you crave. You do not need some external power beyond your control to achieve love and happiness. Indeed, you should rejoice that the power for a good life is in your own hands, and not in some capricious, unpredictable, vain God, as the God of the Bible is made out to be. If you want love, be lovable. If you want happiness, do those things that make you happy and avoid the people who bring you down.

We're running out of time. Can we get the next question? Yes, over here by the...

248. But Jeremiah... I'm sorry to interrupt... but I have a follow-up question. MANY PEOPLE RELY ON A "HIGHER POWER." FOR EXAMPLE, PEOPLE IN A 12-STEP PROGRAM APPEAL TO THEIR HIGHER POWER FOR STRENGTH TO BREAK THE BONDS OF ADDICTION. IF THEY KNOW THAT GOD WILL NOT INTERVENE TO HELP THEM, WON'T THEY LOSE HOPE?

Why should they lose hope? Why shouldn't they be delighted and encouraged to know that millions of people before them have beaten addiction without God's help, even if they *thought* God *was* helping? The "higher power" they seek is inside each person already. Lots of people who could use help worry that they may have flubbed their chance, that they are not "worthy" to be helped.

God wants them to know that they have nothing to worry about. God is not a caseworker reviewing applications for assistance and deciding whom to help. No one who needs help gets turned down. Of course, no one gets any help from God, either. Nearly everyone already possesses the power to help himself or herself. They need not hope or wait for cosmic intervention.

249. WHERE DO WE GO FROM HERE?
Usually, Starbucks®.

Speaking of which, I must be getting back to my regular duties, so we have time for one last question. How about something that will let us go out with a bang? Not a Big Bang, just an ordinary Earth-sized bang.

250. DOES GOD HAVE ANY ADVICE FOR US HUMANS?
Of course.

The first piece of advice is to stop looking for ways to divide yourselves from each other. Especially, stop using your misguided ideas about God as an excuse for division. You Earthlings have more in common with each other than you realize. Consider the vastness of the cosmos, and the fact that there are other beings out there whom you will never know, even if eventually you do manage to contact a few of them. How can you, with this knowledge, continue to draw boundaries and try to keep other Earth people "over there?" When groups of people create "nations," they are creating artificial boundaries and harmful divisions. They are not seeing the big picture. To God, the only natural boundary is the Earth's atmosphere, the void of deep space that naturally separates Earth people from beings elsewhere in the universe. But on the Earth itself, there are no natural boundaries, not even the oceans. God expects you to find the things that unite you as one people – the way God sees you – instead of the things that let you destroy each other and the rest of God's creations.

It seems you hate genocide so much you are willing to go to war against those who commit genocide, like Hitler and Saddam Hussein. So, my second piece of advice is to recognize that you have only two choices to make for the future:

a) Accept severe, worldwide restrictions that naturally and gradually reduce your overpopulation, especially by providing contraceptives and education in your less-wealthy countries, or

b) Accept that without restrictions on the rate of conception, there will have to be reasonably frequent genocides and horrendous epidemics around the planet in order to prevent mass extinction from fights over vital resources.

<u>Third, stop concerning yourself with other people's happiness.</u> It's not your responsibility to make everyone else happy, and it's not your fault and something you need to put an end to if someone else *is* happy.

<u>Fourth, don't worry about the unknowable, and don't waste time thinking about it.</u>

Fifth, do not "put God first," as many would admonish you. Instead, <u>put God's *creations* first.</u> God will exist forever, even after your planet turns to cosmic dust, so God does not need your adulation. But if you don't preserve humanity by treating each other with respect, and if you mistreat your air and water and soil and all other things on Earth, then it – and you – won't exist much longer.

Finally, <u>stop worshipping God, pleading with God, demanding of God.</u> You have all the tools within you that you need for happiness and long life. God gave you those tools, the intellectual, emotional, and physical instruments to control your own lives. Use these resources, and stop trying to find some supernatural cause of and solution to your problems.

Oh, wait, that *wasn't* the final thing. THIS is the definite last advice from God. *Please* stop using the expression "Time flies when you're having fun." God, after all, *is* time, and so there's just something a little creepy about that expression.

And also stop saying "the fullness of time." Same reason.

Now, I can see that several of you will be in trouble if you don't get your coffee and doughnuts transfusion soon. The staff has fixed you a wonderful little reception for your hard work. I'm very grateful to you members of the press for the deep thought that went into your questions and for remaining calm.

So, let's wrap up the press conference right here. We were surprised that no one here asked us to clear up a number of issues. Perhaps we can hold another press conference before you take your next evolutionary step. I leave you now to ponder what questions you might ask then. Thank you, and goodbye.

POSTWORD
FROM JEFFREY MELVIN HUTCHINS

You may wonder who or what Jeremiah is. Is he an angel? An Earthling given extraordinary powers and extended, if not infinite, life? A ghost? God in disguise?

Jeremiah's exact nature must remain part of the mystery of the cosmos, but we will tell you a little about him. He is not a human male, although he may appear that way to you. Jeremiah is not an angel, either, or a ghost. If all creation is a part of God, Jeremiah is that part that can communicate the will of the cosmos in terms that humans can understand. God cannot "talk" in anything like language, but that does not mean God is without some structure (for lack of a better word) that can be described.

Not everything about God can be put in human terms, but Jeremiah was here to help you make sense of some of it.

Philosophy, most people wrongly presume, is harmless. "It's just words." Yet philosophical debate and conclusions have been the basis for much of the hatred and hurt in the world. Philosophy, therefore, probably does not belong in the hands of amateurs like myself.

If you disagree with any portion of the press conference, tell me about it in a respectful way, and I will be respectful in return. (Please go to www.apressconference.com to file your comments.) The answers from "God" in this book are my idea of what a thinking God *might* say, though I don't believe that kind of a God exists. If you have a different idea, then write your own book. Your ideas are just as valid as mine. Maybe.

Consider what "faith" is. We all believe things because they make sense to us, not because there is any empirical evidence that we are right. The explanation each of us has for

- the universe,
- the Earth,
- life, and
- our place in all of those things

is something we take on faith. (Even the atheist, by that definition, has faith.) I respect what others accept as truth. Neither they nor I took on our beliefs in order to spite other people or make fun of them. We hold onto those beliefs that stick in our minds, that seem to help us make the most sense of all we experience, that guide us through the rough spots in our lives. My mind and my heart may be satisfied by different ideas about life than your mind and heart. Neither of us can claim to be more accurate than the other, because neither of us can prove who is right. If we COULD prove it, we wouldn't need faith.

ACKNOWLEDGEMENTS

This book would not have been possible without the support and encouragement of the wonderful community of people at the Unitarian Universalist Church of the North Hills in Pittsburgh, Pennsylvania. They contributed many of the questions to God, and gave me the courage to try to turn a short performance into something more.

Questions in this book came from the following people from all over the country and from every walk of life. In alphabetical order, they are:

Peter Adams, Tom Allen, Sue Amos, Doris Armstrong, Kristine Autenreith, Barbara Barnes, Ron Boyd, John Brobst, Janis Buno-Mociolek, Sylvia Campbell, Debby Camponella, Deb Chaney, Margaret Chonko, Walter Clement, Nancy Cohen, Prescott Cole, Amy Collins, Greg Dietz, Dianne Digianantonio, Jane Dirks, Dolores Donaldson, Jean Dye, John Engberg, Ruth Ernsberger, Bob Ford, Sy Friedman, Leslie Geissler, Kathy Gordon, Eva Goubert, Isaac Goubert, Doris Griffin, Josiah Gromley, Calvin Hadidian, John Hall, Steve Hartlaub, Robert Heasley, Charles Henry, Nancé Hinnenkamp, Dr. Barry Hirsch, Hetty Hirschman, Beth Houseknecht, Robbie Houseknecht, Bill Huckabee, Paula Hurst, Judy Johnson, Paul Johnson, Barbara Jones, Bob Keith, Marty Keith, Abby Lammert, Hazel Leroy, Fran Lynch, Pamela Marques, Karen McCulloch, Audrey McElwain, Roberta Moore, Kevin Nelson, Tracy Nelson, Duane Nichols, Richard Noreikis, Tracy Novak, Tom Nowak, Jean Ogawa, Monty Ogawa, Irene Paul, Leonard Paul, Carl Petrie, Nancy Petrie, Tony Picozzi, Cathy (not to be confused with Carolyn) Pschirer, Kassie Radford, Kelly Radford, Robert Radford, Val Ramsay, Gail Rappolt, Sid Reger, Connie Ritzert, Philip Rivers, Lois Ruskin, Andy Schwarz, Charlie Scott, Richard Scott, Don Shepherd, Deb Shumard, Michael Sicilano, Pauline Simms, Bob Sims, Ann Sitrin, Glenn Solomon, Bob Sproul, Cyd Stackhouse, Jane Switzer, Bob Taft, Carolyn Taft, Beverly Taylor, Craig Thomson, Jill Thomson, Tim Versteeg, Jeanne Walton, Ian Michael Wymbs, Jeanne Zang, Harmon Ziegler, Wayne Zimmerman, and the UUCNH Youth Group.

Much help came in the form of encouragement and discussion about the issues raised in this book. I'd especially like to thank (again in alphabetical order) Elaine Barch, Lou Bartolomucci, Sandi and Howard Belfor, Jim Bernauer, Marty and Hilde Block, Jan Cohen, Jim Crawford, Pat Deines-Marquart, Dennis and Mary Doubleday, David Goldach, Thomas R. Johnson, Joe and Mary Jo Karlovits, John Kichi, Jo Kubesh, Rik Laird, Deloris Lowman, Peter and Molly Lundquist, Tom Meade, the Rev. Carol Meyer, Dan Moore, Susan Mullin, Crysta Ojers, Pat Prozzi, John and Connie Ritzert, Elaine Rose, Janet and Thaddeus Rude, Jim Ruhwedel, Deborah Schuster, Deedee Sprecher, Gina Hillier, Emmanuel Viroux, and everyone else who let me go on thinking I was doing something worthwhile.

Production of this book could not have occurred without the talents and enthusiasm of Virginia Cuenca, Lee Ann Heltzel, and Gina Hillier.

Dr. Joyce Starr deserves my eternal (well, as much eternity as I can control) gratitude for her role in pushing me forward and in convincing me that it would be worth the effort. She is a very special person blessed with enormous insight and humanity, and I encourage you all to buy *her* book "Faxes and Emails to God" now that you've finished this one!

Of course, I cannot end my list of helpers without mentioning my family. My wife Diane, and our two daughters, Rachel and Nell, have been so supportive and encouraging and witty and wonderful. Without their love and support, I would never have completed this book.

ABOUT THE AUTHOR

Jeffrey Melvin Hutchins is a man of many talents who has squandered most of them. He has lived since 1948 against all odds, thanks primarily to the good sense of Diane, his wife since 1971, and his daughters Rachel and Nell. A list of Jeff's accomplishments suggests he has been successful, yet we all know he could have done so much more.

Born in The Bronx, he was raised (as a Unitarian, no less) in Saudi Arabia and Lebanon till age 18, when he "attended" Boston University and got a degree in Broadcasting and Film. For most of his career, he has "worked" in the field of TV captioning, and is now chairman of the Accessible Media Industry Coalition, assuming it has not, as you read this, become defunct due to his inept leadership.

He lives in Pittsburgh, and for many years has been an active member of the Unitarian Universalist Church of the North Hills, no matter what they tell you. Jeff is also a frequent speaker at many UU congregations, though few of them are willing to admit it.

Mostly to pad his résumé, Jeff is currently a member of the Boards of Trustees of the Western Pennsylvania School for the Deaf and the American Community School at Beirut, Lebanon, and a member of the National Advisory Group at the National Technical Institute for the Deaf, a college of the Rochester Institute of Technology. He encourages you to support all of these fine institutions instead of wasting further money on books like this one.

ABOUT THE COVER
Cover design by Lee Ann Fortunato-Heltzel
"Seal of God" design by Virginia Cuenca

INDEX

"666" 184

"Close Encounters of the
 Third Kind" 63

"Da Vinci Code, The" 198

"Dating Game, The".........58

"Fear Factor" 110

"Godfather, The" 170

"It's a Wonderful Life" ..150

"Last Supper, The" 198

"MacArthur Park" 132

"Neverending Story, The"
 ....109, 196

"Onward Christian Soldiers"
195

"Pittsburgh Post-Gazette"14

"Star Wars"......................63

"Survivor" 58

"Ten Commandments, The"
196

"Upstairs, Downstairs".....74

"West Wing, The"..........127

"Wizard of Oz, The"......167,
 253

Abortion...................217, 229

Adam and Eve 140, 147,
 211-213

Afterlife......81, 89, 105, 111,
 113, 115, 120, 123

Aging.........................87, 105

Agnostic............................20

AIDS.........................44, 225

Alcohol............183, 217, 241

Aliens.................63, 66, 122

Allah 126, 163, 179

America..163, 196, 199, 200,
 236, 247, 248

Angelou, Maya 141

Angels..35, 37, 81, 119, 127,
 150, 202

Animals....12, 32, 35, 39, 46,
 56, 60, 67, 68, 74, 80, 81,
 87, 100, 120, 126, 135,
 148, 154, 174, 192, 222,
 230, 233, 240, 241, 250

Apocalypse........................92

Ashcroft, John.................201

Astrology........................200

Atheism...................125, 168

Atheists......20, 24, 125, 128,
 146, 156, 158, 202, 260

Attila the Hun.................199

Aung San Suu Kyi 141

Baptists 206

Batman............................162

Baum, L. Frank...............167

Benedict XVI 161

Berra, Yogi 216

Bible 3, 5, 12, 29, 49,
 51, 65, 99, 132-134, 144,
 146-149, 151, 153-155,
 167, 186, 211, 212, 253

Big Bang ..29, 49, 54-56, 87

Bin Laden, Osama...205, 206

Black hole 52, 84

Blasphemy 150, 233

Blorph 25, 131

Bombs 173, 175, 181, 204

Brando, Marlon 170

Brooks, Mel 126

Brown, Dan.....................198

Buchanan, Pat...................54

Buddha...................142, 216

Buddhists ..47, 135, 156, 179

Bugs 45, 50, 62, 118, 176, 240

Bush, George W. 201, 204- 206

Cannes Film Festival........53

Cats 60

Catholics ...47, 153, 156, 198

Chicago Cubs..................177

Children.......33, 44, 59, 134, 146, 168, 185, 217, 231, 233, 236, 238, 251

Christianity.....................133

Christians.......139, 140, 156, 159, 164, 179

Church..3, 34, 101, 117, 130, 135, 153, 261

Cinderella.......................219

Cloning 46, 229

Coincidence...........38, 45, 85

Commandments.......38, 149, 150, 206, 221

Communism....................167

Conception.....145, 217, 244, 255

Contraceptives........239, 255

Cook, Peter 196

Creationists.............213, 246

Crusades 156

Cults...............................132

Deus ex machina...............180

Devil 37, 38, 84, 119, 194, 196

Dirty Harry 210

Disease.........21, 44, 48, 112, 154, 190, 191, 229, 236

Diversity....44, 64, 101, 135, 195

DNA............48, 50, 179, 231

Dogs......38, 60, 62, 119, 223

Don Corleone 170

Doomsday........................95

Downey, Roma 150

Drugs................87, 183, 200

Dullea, Keir....................196

Earle, Steve....................194

Earth ..15, 19, 21, 32, 36, 40, 44, 46, 51, 56, 57, 60-64, 66-68, 72, 80, 92, 94, 95, 98-100, 103, 107, 108, 118-120, 122, 124, 131, 132, 135, 137, 140, 143, 146, 153, 156, 157, 165, 166, 169, 181, 185, 187, 191, 192, 201, 203, 206, 211-213, 222, 228, 231, 232, 237, 239, 240, 241, 245, 249, 250, 251, 255, 256, 260

Earthquake 179

Egypt 149, 151

Egyptians..........31, 151, 194

Einstein, Albert 29, 78, 88

Email..................................15

Environment..44, 56, 62, 63, 66, 80, 81, 98, 100, 126, 135, 157, 168, 174, 185, 192, 199, 233, 235, 248

Evil 23, 35, 37, 84, 120, 121, 133, 174, 187, 189, 208, 212, 250

Evolution 44, 45, 60, 66, 69, 99, 101, 102, 124, 136, 154, 169, 193, 213, 227, 229, 237, 246

Faith........3, 20, 21, 103, 125, 128, 131, 164, 201, 260

Faith healers....................164

Falwell, Jerry..........139, 225

Family 70, 81, 107, 112, 148, 153, 175, 207, 216

Father 40, 140, 149, 153, 180

Food.......14, 48, 66, 95, 176, 180, 240, 245

Freedom...... 22, 39, 84, 210, 242

Freethinkers 47

Freud, Sigmund.................38

Fundamentalists 146, 167

Gamblers 158

Gandhi, Mohandas 210

Gays 156, 169, 220, 225, 226

Gender......................13, 244

Genesis 49, 212

Ghosts.............................122

Gibran, Kahlil 229

Gknisfudn Galaxy 57, 131

Golden Rule......80, 223, 228

Gore, Al 199

Gospel music 117

Graffiti 144

Gravity ...12, 39, 54, 57, 96, 99

Greeks......................31, 127

Happiness 40, 113, 191, 214, 253, 256

Heaven.............24, 37, 81, 92, 113-115, 117-120, 170, 202, 219, 236

Hell 34, 35, 37, 113, 117-121, 202, 214

Heston, Charlton 196

Hindus 47

Hitchcock, Alfred..............82

Hitler 95, 176, 186, 187, 199, 250, 255

Hobby 15

Holy Grail.......................152

Homosexuality....... 219-221, 223, 225

Hunger....................118, 124

I Ching...............................5

Ice Age.............................17

Idiots...............................178

Infinity..........19, 29, 31, 184

Intelligent design 45

Interconnected Web.........44

Internet............................133

Islam 133

Israel 76, 151

Jesus 125, 139, 140-144, 152, 198, 216

Jews..47, 139, 156, 157, 179, 186, 187

Jordan, Michael 141

Judaism 133

Judge Judy 91

Jung, Carl..........................38

Khadafi, Moammar.........225

Khmer Rouge..................167

Kilmer, Joyce 46

Knopfler, Mark 194

Koran 5, 133, 144, 155

Language 17, 18, 27, 63, 103, 134, 143, 169, 211, 213, 248

Lean Cuisine® 145

Lee, Peggy 194

Leno, Jay.........................210

Limbaugh, Rush 50
Little League 159
Love ...21, 25, 29, 32, 58, 74,
   99, 118, 123, 124, 165,
   170, 185, 190, 215, 216,
   221, 223, 226, 227, 245,
   253
Lucas, George.................184
Mandela, Nelson.............141
Marriage..14, 218, 219, 221,
   222, 226
   Gay 225, 226
Mary 140, 144
Mary Magdalene 198
Mason, Jackie.................149
Meditation 200
Merlin 52
Microsoft® 50
Middle East 90, 238
Miracle....................153, 154
Missionaries......................32
Money.....117, 200, 203, 207
Monogamy......................227
Monty Python 126
Moore, Demi...................196
Moore, Dudley...............196
Mormons 47
Moses..... ..38, 149-151, 206,
   221
Mother..33, 40, 81, 149, 217
Mother-in-law, crazed......33
Movies 40, 96, 171, 189,
   195-197, 208, 231
MTV 145
Muhammad.....................142
Murder......21, 175, 199, 209
Murphy, Bridey 121

Music 18, 57, 63, 72, 99,
   130, 194, 195
Muslims ...47, 156, 163, 164,
   206
Nader, Ralph...................141
Nicholson, Jack 21
Niebuhr, Reinhold 203
Noah 148
Norsemen.........................31
Pagan 179
Paparazzi 34
Pavlov, Ivan....................119
Peace....89, 94, 96, 113, 182,
   185
PEZ®..............................191
Pharaoh............149, 151, 187
Plants ...…...12, 44, 46, 56, 67,
   68, 74, 81, 113, 126, 135,
   177, 192, 233
Pol Pot............................199
Pollution 98
Pope 161
Popeye 201
Population 66, 94, 95,
   237-239, 255
Pornography....................231
Powerball®.....................145
Prayer 23, 84, 101, 158,
   159, 161-164, 167, 170,
   177, 205
Procreation 222, 243
Prophets. 143, 165-167,
   169
Proteins 50
Protestants 47
Psychic Friends 199
Psychics 175
PwiQtlspa 152

Queen of Heaven 13
Ratzinger, Joseph 161
Red Sea 149, 151
Reese, Della 150
Regret 66, 112
Reincarnation 89, 121
Rocks 62, 108, 135, 172, 173
Roddenberry, Gene 184
Romans 31, 127
Runyon, Damon..............249
Rushdie, Salman 5
Salvation 214
Santa Claus 73, 158, 159, 202
Sarandon, Susan 141
SARS.................................44
Satan 37, 84
Scrabble® 25
Sex 100, 125, 140, 211, 218, 220-224, 231, 232, 241, 242, 244
Shroud of Turin..............144
Sickness...........................124
Simon, Carly 194
Sin 49, 120, 147, 210, 211, 213, 214
Sleep........16, 38, 78, 81, 116
Socialism..........................167
Spielberg, Steven 242
Starbucks® 254
Suffering ..22, 104, 118, 187, 236
Suicide.................76, 87, 175
Superstition 46, 100, 247
Taliban.............................167
Taoists 135
Teenagers 27, 114, 211

Television 57, 69, 71, 76, 84, 92, 161, 193, 195, 198, 231
Ten Commandments...... See Commandments
Terrorism 120, 121, 163, 204, 215
Tobacco 241
Torah 5, 133, 151, 155
Travers, Henry...............150
Trinity 139
Tutu, Desmond..............141
Twister® 25
Unitarians...3, 135, 139, 261
Universal Salvation 139
Universalists......3, 135, 139, 261
Velcro®..............................50
Volcano 174
War....11, 25, 40, 74, 89, 95, 96, 99, 171, 172, 177, 178, 180-184, 186, 197, 198, 204, 215, 237, 250
Washington, George......200
Water......44, 50, 66, 95, 96, 98, 100, 111, 135, 148, 151, 228, 237, 238
Weapons ..74, 155, 172, 181, 185
Weather Channel............199
Westheimer, Dr. Ruth......58
White, Barry.....................58
Wilson, Flip.....................37
Worship........19, 32, 74, 77, 130, 168, 194, 206, 210
Wright, Frank Lloyd 58, 154